The I ♥ TRADER JOE'S® PLANT-BASED COOKBOOK

150 Delicious Vegetarian and Vegan Recipes Using Foods from the World's Greatest Grocery Store

KRIS CRAMER

Published by:
Ulysses Press
PO Box 3440
Berkeley, CA 94703
www.ulyssespress.com

ISBN: 978-1-64604-493-1
Library of Congress Control Number: 2023930694

Printed in China
10 9 8 7 6 5 4 3 2 1

Acquisitions editor: Casie Vogel
Managing editor: Claire Chun
Project editor: Paulina Maurovich
Editors: Renee Rutledge, Lauren Harrison, Elyce Berrigan-Dunlop
Proofreader: Michele Anderson
Front cover design: Winnie Liu
Cover artwork: vegetables © mamita/shutterstock.com; photos © Kris Cramer
Interior artwork: see page 204
Production: Yesenia Garcia-Lopez

Contents

MAIN DISHES 124

CASSEROLES 144

DESSERTS

BEVERAGES

SAMPLE MENUS

CONVERSIONS

PHOTO CREDITS

RECIPE INDEX

ACKNOWLEDGMENTS

ABOUT THE AUTHOR

Introduction

When you say the words "Trader Joe's" to a TJ's lover, there's a consistent reaction. Their eyes go soft, the corners of their mouth creep up into an unconscious smile, and they will, undoubtedly, make a contented noise of happiness laced with "yum." Smaller than a traditional grocery store, with oddly packaged food and an offbeat aesthetic, Trader Joe's is truly an experience—an experience that has won the hearts of millions of faithful shoppers.

What is it about Joe's that makes it so magical? First off, the prices can't be beat. You don't need coupons or sales to get the best price at TJ's—there's a no-haggling policy. The best price is presented up front with no clubs to join or hoops to jump through—it's a nice change. Trader Joe's works from a unique model: The company purchases products you're likely familiar with from other retailers, except it buys them directly from producers, rather than going through a distributor, like other retailers do. Cutting out the middleman lets TJ's build a relationship with these producers and lowers the cost of the items because the producers can now offer larger quantities of their product. As a result of this direct relationship and the cost-savings, most of the products are repackaged in TJ's quirky packaging. By using the TJ's packaging, the producers have the benefit of offering their goods to a greater audience, but they lessen their risk of competing against themselves at the other stores. There are even some items that are distributed exclusively by Trader Joe's, typically seasonal and imported items that have limited runs.

Despite being a chain, Trader Joe's is a privately held company. Because they don't have stockholders to appease, they're able to do things a little differently. Although they aren't franchised, the company recognizes how important it is to connect to the community. With their well-trained and caring staff, they work to be a neighborhood market. In your local Trader Joe's, you're likely to see murals of local points of interest painted on the walls. Additionally, TJ's builds relationships with local farms and bakeries in their respective neighborhoods, bringing business to the community and bringing you fresh, quality food.

I'm a longtime lover of Joe's and my praises of the store on my blog have, over the years, garnered some disbelief. I've even been asked if I was being paid to advertise for them—I wish! While it can seem too good to be true, this sort of fervent passion is just what happens to Trader Joe's customers. The store's unique products, high-quality standards, and happy staff create the perfect recipe for an exceptional shopping experience. When you have that sort of dynamic, no bribery is needed—the love TJ's instills in its customers inspires them to willingly, and happily, preach the good word.

TRADER JOE'S QUALITY

Trader Joe's is known for its quality standards, which far surpass anything you've seen at most any other grocery store. No GMOs, no added hydrogenated fats, no food coloring...it's quite impressive and assures you that you're feeding your family quality food.

In addition to the general quality standards, TJ's also has some wonderful labeling practices. Many house products are labeled with easy-to-read symbols, denoting which products are vegetarian, vegan, gluten-free, or low sodium, or fall under a host of other categories.

One thing to note, however, is that items are not always marked with all the categories they fall into. For example, the semisweet chocolate chips are vegan, but marked only as being gluten-free. This is why I recommended grabbing one of their handy product guides. Available both in-store and online, they list all of the items that are vegan, vegetarian, and gluten-free.

If you have dietary restrictions, always be sure to read the label. Distributors, manufacturing processes, and recipes change, and regional differences occur—all important things to consider, regardless of where you shop.

A NOTE ON ALL THINGS VEGAN

There are differing standards in determining whether a product is truly vegan. Some things that are important to strict vegans are not as important to other vegans. In that light, I want to be clear about some of the products used in this book and their relationship to vegan dietary guidelines.

For many vegans, the source of sugar in an item is a key determinant because most sugar is refined using a charcoal filter, and charcoal can be considered an animal by-product. Not all vegans observe this and for the purposes of this book, the source of sugar is not something that I concerned myself with. There are certain things used in this book (such as boxed baking mixes) that, when prepared in the way I instruct, become vegan baked goods, but the source of the sugar in the mix is not determined.

Additionally, while Trader Joe's is a phenomenal store, it doesn't have the endless breadth of options one might find at a conventional grocery store. In that case, there are certain items listed in the vegan options, such as vegan puff pastry or vegan cheese, that will have to be located at other stores. However, you'll find that the majority of the vegan alternatives listed are readily available at your local TJ's.

RENNET AND CHEESE

Rennet is an enzyme that goes into cheesemaking. It can come from one of three sources: animal (intestines), microbial, or plants. Often, the ingredient list simply refers to it as "rennet," leaving the cheese buyer unaware of the rennet's source.

Thankfully, Trader Joe's labels the source of rennet on their ingredients. Additionally, you can get in-store information on which cheeses use microbial rennet and which use animal rennet, important for vegetarians who eat dairy. I recommend double-checking the source when you shop at different locations, as many of their cheeses vary by region. Information on their nationally carried cheeses is available in their handy product guides.

PRODUCT AVAILABILITY

Sometimes the day comes when you visit your beloved Trader Joe's and a product you've come to rely on is no longer on the shelf. "Perhaps they're just out," you think. Sometimes that's just it—they are out. But occasionally the item in question is gone, not because of a back stock issue, but because it's been diskontinued. This can cause panic, but never fear! Check with your friendly Hawaiian shirts, because they may have more information. For example, some items (like Pumpkin Pie Spice) are seasonal—so they are temporarily gone, but not forgotten. And if the product you seek has, in fact, crossed over the rainbow bridge, there's a good chance that something new and magical has also entered the store, something delicious that you might love even more.

And not to get your hopes up, but I have seen long-lost favorites (including my beloved Valencia peanut butter!) make returns after indefinite time off the shelf. You never know what will happen, only that it's sure to be delicious.

WHAT DOES IT MEAN?: A NOTE ON OIL AND VINEGAR

"Mild vinegar": When mild vinegar is noted, it means a lightly flavored vinegar such as white distilled or apple cider vinegar.

"Mild vegetable oil": Mild vegetable oil denotes a vegetable oil that is virtually flavorless and suitable for cooking and baking, such as canola, grapeseed, or a vegetable blend.

"Olive oil": Ooh, mama. Trader Joe's is the land of high-quality olive oils that are actually—gasp—affordable. The selection can vary and so will your budget and taste, so I keep it general so you can insert your preferred oil of choice. Unless it suits the recipe, I would stick with a plain olive oil and avoid infused varieties like garlic.

Breakfast

Call it breakfast, brunch, or brinner (breakfast-for-dinner)—anyway you cut it, it's my favorite meal of the day. This chapter is full of recipes to please sweet and savory breakfast lovers alike, running the gamut from quick meals to lovingly prepared spreads for your family to feast upon. The one thing they all have in common is that they're chock-full of delicious ingredients your family will happily wake up for.

- BANANA CINNAMON ROLLS
- PEANUT BUTTER CREAM CHEESE FROSTING
- ORANGE-BLUEBERRY CORNBREAD MUFFINS
- WILD RICE BREAKFAST PORRIDGE
- ORANGE CREAMSICLE COFFEE CAKE
- BLUEBERRY CRUMB CAKE
- PINEAPPLE UPSIDE-DOWN PANCAKES
- SAVORY MUFFINS
- BREAKFAST COOKIES
- TASTY TOFU SCRAMBLE
- QUINOA BREAKFAST BREAD
- CINN-AGAVE PB SPREAD
- APPLE OATMEAL PARFAIT
- QUICK AND DIRTY DANISH
- A TALE OF TWO FRENCH TOASTS
- SPICED APRICOT OATS
- SAVORY BREAKFAST ROLLS
- CRANBERRY BANANA OATMEAL MUFFINS
- THE ULTIMATE WAFFLE

BANANA CINNAMON ROLLS

Oh, lordy. These rolls are moist and tender and filled with banana and cinnamon. You'll never again be satisfied by regular cinnamon rolls after tasting these beauties. Add a healthy smear of Peanut Butter Cream Cheese Frosting and they'll easily prove to be the most redonkulous things you've ever tasted.

ROLLS:

1 (¼-ounce) packet active dry yeast (about 2¼ teaspoons)

¼ cup warm water

½ teaspoon Trader Joe's Organic Evaporated Cane Juice Sugar

3 tablespoons melted unsalted butter

¼ cup warm milk

2 tablespoons Trader Joe's Organic Maple Agave Syrup Blend

1 cup mashed ripe banana

4 to 5 cups unbleached all-purpose flour

FILLING:

6 tablespoons Trader Joe's Organic Evaporated Cane Juice Sugar

2 teaspoons ground cinnamon

1 large ripe banana, thinly sliced

5 tablespoons cold unsalted butter

1½ cups Peanut Butter Cream Cheese Frosting (recipe follows)

To make the rolls: In a large bowl, combine the yeast, warm water, and sugar. Swirl the mixture together and let it sit to proof the yeast. It will become thick and cloudy. Add the butter, milk, maple-agave syrup, and mashed banana, and mix well. One cup at a time, incorporate the flour until a dough comes together. The dough should be tacky. Knead until elastic, about 5 minutes. Place the dough in a lightly oiled bowl. Cover with a kitchen towel and let the dough rise until doubled, about 1 hour.

To make the filling: In a small bowl, combine the sugar and cinnamon. Turn out the dough onto a lightly floured surface and gently knead. Roll out the dough into a 12 x 18-inch rectangle. Sprinkle the cinnamon topping over the surface. Spread out the banana slices randomly on top of the cinnamon. Cut the cold butter into small bits and sprinkle them randomly on top. Roll the dough tightly into a log beginning from the long edge. Cut the dough into 12 even slices and arrange the rolls in an ungreased 8 x 11-inch pan. Cover and let the dough rise until the rolls are doubled, about 1 hour.

Preheat oven to 375°F. Bake the rolls, uncovered, for 20 minutes, or until golden. Let them cool slightly and frost with the Peanut Butter Cream Cheese Frosting before serving.

MAKES: 12 rolls

VEGAN OPTION: Use nondairy milk and Trader Joe's Vegan Buttery Spread in place of the dairy equivalents.

PEANUT BUTTER CREAM CHEESE FROSTING

This frosting is pure bliss. Just nutty enough, not too sweet, and oh so creamy. Spread it on Banana Cinnamon Rolls (page 13).

4 ounces cream cheese

2 to 3 tablespoons Trader Joe's Organic Creamy Salted Peanut Butter

4 to 5 tablespoons Trader Joe's Organic Powdered Sugar

splash of milk

In a medium bowl, beat the cream cheese and the peanut butter with a handheld mixer on medium speed. Add the powdered sugar until the frosting is to your desired sweetness. If the frosting gets too thick, add a splash of milk to smooth it out.

MAKES: 1¼ to 1½ cups of frosting

VEGAN OPTION: Substitute nondairy cream cheese and nondairy milk in place of the dairy ingredients.

ORANGE-BLUEBERRY CORNBREAD MUFFINS

Tender, orange-kissed cornbread muffins bursting with tender blueberries...seriously, does anything sound more delicious than that? These are simple, fast, and tasty—woo-hoo!

juice and grated zest of 1 large orange (about ⅓ cup juice)

¼ cup mild vegetable oil

⅔ cup milk

1 (15-ounce) box Trader Joe's Cornbread Mix

1 cup fresh or frozen blueberries

Preheat the oven to 400°F and line a standard 12-cup muffin tin with liners or lightly grease and flour the cups. In a large bowl, combine the juice, zest, oil, and milk, and whisk to combine. In 2 batches, incorporate the cornbread mix. Gently fold in the blueberries. Spoon the mixture into the muffin cups, filling to just under the rim. Bake until golden and a toothpick inserted into the center of each muffin comes out clean, 15 to 18 minutes.

MAKES: 12 muffins

VEGAN OPTION: Substitute a nondairy milk for the dairy milk.

WILD RICE BREAKFAST PORRIDGE

This dish is based on a delicious breakfast porridge served at a popular Minneapolis restaurant. My version increases the heartiness while drastically lowering the fat. This porridge is highly addictive, so I suggest making a large batch. It keeps well in the fridge over the course of a couple of days.

2 cups milk

½ cup Trader Joe's Rolled Oats

1 cup cooked Trader Joe's Wild Rice

2 to 3 tablespoons Trader Joe's Organic Maple Agave Syrup Blend

¼ teaspoon vanilla extract

3 to 4 tablespoons dried cranberries

3 to 4 tablespoons chopped hazelnuts

½ cup fresh blueberries

In a large saucepan over medium heat, bring the milk to a simmer, being mindful not to let it boil. Add the oats and reduce the heat to medium low. Cook, stirring often, until thick, about 5 minutes. Add the wild rice and continue to cook until the porridge thickens a bit more (it will still be a little soupy) and the wild rice heats through, about 5 minutes. Add the maple-agave syrup and vanilla, adjusting syrup to taste. Remove from the heat. Divide the porridge among 2 bowls and evenly top with cranberries, hazelnuts, and blueberries. Serve warm, with extra maple-agave syrup, if desired.

MAKES: 2 servings

VEGAN OPTION: Replace the milk with a nondairy milk of your choice.

ORANGE CREAMSICLE COFFEE CAKE

With an abundance of orange zest, along with fresh orange juice, this cake is both fragrant and has a tender crumb. Try it "breakfast a la mode"—with a dollop of Greek yogurt on top.

TOPPING:

¼ cup unbleached all-purpose flour

3 tablespoons Trader Joe's Organic Evaporated Cane Juice Sugar

3 tablespoons cold unsalted butter

¼ cup Trader Joe's Raw Silvered Almond

CAKE:

2¼ cups unbleached all-purpose flour

¾ cup Trader Joe's Organic Evaporated Cane Juice Sugar

2 teaspoons baking powder

½ teaspoon baking soda

¼ teaspoon salt

juice and grated zest of 2 large oranges (about ⅔ cup juice)

⅓ cup mild oil

⅓ cup milk

2 teaspoons vanilla extract

Heat the oven to 400°F and lightly grease and flour a 9-inch square baking pan. Line the bottom with parchment paper, if using.

To make the topping: In a small bowl, combine the flour and sugar. Cut in the butter with a pastry cutter or the back of a fork until a clumpy, mealy mixture comes together. Add the almonds. Refrigerate to keep cold.

To make the cake: In a large bowl, combine the flour, sugar, baking powder, baking soda, and salt. In a second large bowl, whisk together the fresh orange juice and zest, oil, milk, and vanilla. Add the dry ingredients to the wet ingredients in 2 batches, mixing until just combined. Spread the batter in the prepared pan and sprinkle with the topping. Bake until a toothpick inserted into the center comes out clean, 32 to 35 minutes.

MAKES: 8 to 10 slices of cake

....

VEGAN OPTION: Replace the butter with Trader Joe's Vegan Buttery Spread and use a nondairy milk of your choice.

....

BLUEBERRY CRUMB CAKE

Crumb cake so good, you'll want to smack someone! But that would be terribly mean, so give them a piece of this moist, berry-studded cake with a lovely crumb topping and smack your lips instead. Fresh berries are best in this recipe, but frozen are fine.

CRUMB TOPPING:

½ cup unbleached all-purpose flour

¼ cup Trader Joe's Organic Evaporated Cane Juice Sugar

¼ cup cold unsalted butter (or margarine)

CAKE:

3 cups unbleached all-purpose flour

1⅓ cups Trader Joe's Organic Evaporated Cane Juice Sugar

1 tablespoon baking powder

¼ teaspoon salt

2 cups milk

1 teaspoon mild vinegar

½ cup mild oil

1½ teaspoon vanilla extract

2 cups blueberries

Preheat the oven to 400°F and lightly grease and flour a 10- to 12-cup tube cake pan, such as a Bundt pan.

To make the topping: In a small bowl, combine the flour and sugar. Cut in the butter or margarine with a pastry cutter or the back of a fork until a clumpy, mealy mixture comes together. Refrigerate to keep cold.

To make the cake: In a medium bowl, stir together the flour, sugar, baking powder, and salt. In a second large bowl, combine the milk and vinegar and let the mixture sit for a minute. Add the oil and vanilla. In 2 batches, add the dry ingredients to the wet ingredients until just mixed. Gently fold in the blueberries and then spread the batter in the pan. Top with the crumb topping. Bake until golden and a toothpick inserted into the center comes out clean, 40 to 45 minutes. Let the cake cool completely in the pan before gently loosening the cake from the pan with a knife and removing.

MAKES: 12 to 16 slices of cake

VEGAN OPTION: Replace the butter with Trader Joe's Vegan Buttery Spread and use a nondairy milk of your choice.

PINEAPPLE UPSIDE-DOWN PANCAKES

Buttery pineapple-encrusted pancakes with tender crumbs are basically the best thing ever. You can pair them with a shmear of cherry jam or go traditional with syrup; either way, they will taste incredible. The oats bring a little oomph to the batter without adding any texture, so don't worry about the pancakes tasting grainy—they melt in your mouth like buttah.

1½ cups unbleached all-purpose flour

¼ cup Trader Joe's Rolled Oats

1 tablespoon baking powder

⅛ teaspoon salt

1¼ to 1½ cups milk

¼ cup water

2 tablespoons Trader Joe's Organic Maple Agave Syrup Blend

1 tablespoon mild vegetable oil

½ teaspoon vanilla extract

1½ cups Trader Joe's Pineapple Tidbits, thawed and chopped

mild oil, as needed

In a large bowl, combine the flour, oats, baking powder, and salt. In second large bowl, combine the milk, water, maple-agave syrup, oil, and vanilla, and stir to combine. Add the wet ingredients to dry ingredients and whisk until just mixed—the batter may be a little lumpy and that's fine. Add more milk if needed; you want the batter to spread easily, but not be too runny. Heat a medium pan or griddle over medium heat with just enough oil to grease the surface. The pan is ready when a drop of water sizzles when dropped into the middle. Ladle on ⅓ cup of the pancake batter and top with 1 to 2 tablespoons of the pineapple. Flip the pancake when the edges look slightly firmed up and it bubbles a little in the middle, 3 to 4 minutes. Cook on the other side until puffy and the pineapple bottom is lightly browned, 2 to 3 minutes. Transfer the cooked pancake to a plate and keep warm in a low oven. Repeat with the rest of the batter. Serve with toppings of your choice.

MAKES: 6 to 7 pancakes

VEGAN OPTION: Replace the milk with a nondairy milk of your choice.

SAVORY MUFFINS

Truly tender and moist, these muffins are not misshapen scones or lazy biscuits. True to all that is muffin-topped and holy, these morsels are full of savory goodness and beg to be slathered with butter. If you make them, your muffin world will be rocked. You have been warned.

2 cups unbleached all-purpose flour

2 tablespoons Trader Joe's Organic Evaporated Cane Juice Sugar

2 teaspoons dried oregano

1 teaspoon garlic powder

1 teaspoon baking powder

½ teaspoon baking soda

¼ teaspoon salt

1¼ cups milk

¼ cup mild vegetable oil

¼ teaspoon mild vinegar

¾ cup Trader Joe's Shredded 3 Cheese Blend

¼ cup chopped Trader Joe's Julienne Sliced Sun Dried Tomatoes, drained

Preheat the oven to 400°F and grease and flour a standard 12-cup muffin tin. In a small bowl, combine the flour, sugar, oregano, garlic powder, baking powder, baking soda, and salt. In a large bowl, combine the milk, oil, and vinegar. Let sit for a minute, then whisk in the cheese and sun-dried tomatoes. In 2 batches, incorporate the dry ingredients into the wet ingredients, mixing until just combined. Spoon the batter into the prepared tin, filling to just under the rim of each cup. Bake until a toothpick inserted into the center comes out clean, 14 to 16 minutes. Let the muffins cool in the tin, on a cooling rack. Store leftover muffins covered at room temperature.

MAKES: 12 muffins

VEGAN OPTION: Replace the milk with a nondairy milk of your choice and the cheddar with a vegan cheese (or omit the cheese altogether).

BREAKFAST COOKIES

Cookies for breakfast?! Heck yeah! After playing around with a handful of ideas, I came up with these soft, chewy cookies that are just sweet enough to classify as a cookie, yet truly hold their own as a highly portable breakfast. Pair with a piece of fruit and perhaps some milk. I promise they will make getting out of bed in the morning a little bit easier. If you'd prefer to use all white whole wheat flour, you can omit the unbleached all-purpose flour and replace it with ½ cup more white whole wheat.

1 cup Trader Joe's Rolled Oats

½ cup white whole wheat flour

½ cup unbleached all-purpose flour

2 tablespoons Trader Joe's Organic Evaporated Cane Juice Sugar

½ teaspoon ground cinnamon

½ teaspoon baking powder

¼ teaspoon salt

2 very ripe bananas, gently mashed but still slightly lumpy

½ cup roasted, salted Trader Joe's Almond Butter

¼ cup vegetable oil

2 tablespoons Trader Joe's Organic Maple Agave Syrup Blend

¼ teaspoon vanilla extract

⅓ cup raisins

Preheat the oven to 350°F and line a baking sheet with parchment paper. In a small bowl, combine the oats, white whole wheat flour, all-purpose flour, sugar, cinnamon, baking powder, and salt. In a large bowl, combine the bananas, almond butter, oil, maple-agave syrup, and vanilla until smooth. Add the dry ingredients in batches, including the raisins in the last batch, and mix until the dough comes together and the dry ingredients are incorporated. Spoon out the dough in large balls, about 2 tablespoons in size, and flatten slightly onto the parchment paper. Bake until set and lightly brown on the edges, 16 to 18 minutes. Let the cookies cool on the baking sheet, on a cooling rack, for 10 minutes before transferring the cookies directly to the rack. If you want to make regular-size cookies, as opposed to extra-large cookies, scoop out 1 tablespoon of dough at a time and reduce the bake time to 10 to 12 minutes.

MAKES: 12 extra-large cookies or 24 regular-size cookies

VARIATION: Mix things up with peanut butter and chocolate chips in place of the almond butter and raisins.

TASTY TOFU SCRAMBLE

This tofu scramble is a staple in my breakfast repertoire. It's simple and very versatile, so you can use up the contents of your vegetable crisper to mix things up.

2 tablespoons olive oil

1 medium yellow onion, diced

1 tablespoon dried oregano

1 tablespoon dried basil

1 (14-ounce) block Trader Joe San Firm Tofu, drained but not pressed

⅓ cup chopped or pureed Trader Joe's Julienne Sliced Sun Dried Tomatoes in Olive Oil

1 large carrot, sliced into thin disks

3 cups Trader Joe's Organics Baby Spinach, rinsed

¼ cup Trader Joe's Organic Super Sweet Cut Corn (in the frozen section)

¼ cup Trader Joe's Pitted Kalamata Olives, chopped

salt and pepper

VEGAN, GLUTEN FREE

In a large pan, heat the oil over medium heat and sauté the onion until translucent, 5 to 8 minutes. Add the oregano and basil and stir to combine, adding a bit more oil if the mixture begins to stick. Crumble the tofu on top and mix well. Add the sun-dried tomatoes and carrot and stir to combine. Top with the spinach and cover with a lid to let the spinach wilt. Reduce the heat to medium low and let cook for about 5 minutes, stirring occasionally. If things start to stick, add a little water, 1 to 2 tablespoons. Stir to incorporate the wilted spinach and add the corn and olives. Continue to cook on low until heated through, about 3 minutes. Season to taste with salt and pepper.

MAKES: 3 to 4 servings

QUINOA BREAKFAST BREAD

Quinoa, almonds, and dried cherries stud this bread, making it a delicious and hearty option for breakfast. It also breathes life into leftover quinoa that's destined for a slow refrigerator death. I like to eat warm slices of it with a little Cinn-Agave PB Spread (recipe follows).

1 cup unbleached all-purpose flour

1 cup white whole wheat flour

½ cup Trader Joe's Organic Evaporated Cane Juice Sugar

1½ teaspoons baking powder

½ teaspoon baking soda

¼ teaspoon salt

1½ cups cooked, cooled quinoa

1 cup plus 2 tablespoons milk

⅓ cup mild vegetable oil

1 teaspoon vanilla extract

½ cup Trader Joe's Raw Blanched Slivered Almonds

½ cup Trader Joe's Dried Pitted Tart Montmorency Cherries

¼ cup semisweet chocolate chips

Preheat the oven to 350°F and lightly grease and flour a standard loaf pan. In a small bowl, combine the all-purpose flour, white whole wheat flour, sugar, baking powder, baking soda, and salt. In a large bowl, whisk together the quinoa, milk, oil, and vanilla. Add the dry ingredients to the wet ingredients in 2 batches until just mixed. Gently mix in the almonds, cherries, and chocolate chips. Bake until a toothpick inserted into the center comes out clean (a few crumbs are okay), 55 to 60 minutes. Let the bread cool in the pan, on a cooling rack, for 30 minutes before serving.

MAKES: 10 to 12 slices of bread

VEGAN OPTION: Replace the milk with a nondairy milk of your choice.

CINN-AGAVE PB SPREAD

This is simple and addictive—you'll be spreading it on EVERYTHING!

½ cup Trader Joe's Creamy Valencia Peanut Butter

2 tablespoons Trader Joe's Organic Maple Agave Syrup Blend

1 teaspoon ground cinnamon

VEGAN, GLUTEN-FREE

In a small bowl, combine the peanut butter and maple-agave syrup until smooth. Mix in the cinnamon and adjust to taste, adding more sweetener or cinnamon as you'd like. The cinnamon will become stronger after sitting. Store the spread in a covered container in the fridge for up to 2 weeks.

MAKES: ½ cup of spread

COOK'S NOTE: You can always try different nut butters; almond or sunflower seed butter would be delicious as well!

APPLE OATMEAL PARFAIT

Trader Joe's is a great place to score a deal on nut butters. This parfait is a perfect way to put your cheap find to use—the melding of almond and apples is heavenly. The almond butter gives this breakfast a healthy fat and protein boost, and the applesauce makes it feel decadent. To add a little texture, I recommend trying the chunky almond butter. Indulge knowing you're nourishing yourself!

Trader Joe's Quick Cook Steel Cut Oats

¼ cup Trader Joe's Crunchy Almond Butter

2 tablespoons Trader Joe's Organic Maple Agave Syrup Blend

sprinkle of ground cinnamon

sprinkle of salt

2 (4-ounce) cups Trader Joe's Applesauce

fresh apple slices or almonds, for garnish (optional)

VEGAN

Cook the oats according to the package directions. Once the oatmeal is prepared, remove it from the heat and stir in the almond butter, maple-agave syrup, cinnamon, and salt. Divide the oatmeal and layer with the applesauce in bowls or cups, alternating a layer of oatmeal with a layer of applesauce. Repeat for 4 or 5 layers, depending on the depth of your serving dishes. Garnish with fresh apple slices or almonds, if using.

MAKES: 2 servings

QUICK AND DIRTY DANISH

This Danish recipe is so simple, it's great to have in your pocket for unexpected guests or rainy, lazy weekend days. The recipe doubles easily, and if you're well stocked with a variety of jams, everyone can have their favorite flavor, so there will be no squabbling. Or if someone gives you sass, just stuff a Danish in their mouth—it works every time.

1 sheet of Trader Joe's Artisan Puff Pastry (in the frozen section)

4 ounces cream cheese

2 tablespoons Trader Joe's Organic Evaporated Cane Juice Sugar

½ teaspoon lemon juice

¼ teaspoon Trader Joe's vanilla extract

2 tablespoons melted unsalted butter

assorted jams or preserves

Preheat the oven to 400°F and line a baking sheet with parchment paper. Cut the frozen puff pastry into 16 (1½-inch) squares. DO NOT ROLL OUT. In a small bowl, beat together the cream cheese, sugar, lemon juice, and vanilla until smooth. Brush each square with the melted butter. Top each square with a tablespoon of the cream cheese mixture, and make an indentation in the top of the cream cheese and add a scant teaspoon of jam. Bake until the edges have puffed up and are golden brown, 12 to 16 minutes. Let the pastries cool for about 5 minutes before serving.

MAKES: 16 Danish pastries

VEGAN OPTION: Replace the puff pastry with a nondairy puff pastry, such as Pepperidge Farm, and substitute soy cream cheese and Trader Joe's Vegan Buttery Spread for the cream cheese and butter.

A TALE OF TWO FRENCH TOASTS

Having to choose between sweet and salty is always the battle of brunch. With this versatile recipe, you can have it both ways. The cinnamon-sugar topping caramelizes into burbled decadence while the everything seasoning melds into the bread, creating the ultimate breakfast treat.

2 eggs

½ cup milk

¼ cup plus 1 tablespoon Trader Joe's Organic Evaporated Cane Juice Sugar, divided

1 teaspoon Trader Joe's Organic Ground Cinnamon

1 loaf Trader Joe's Challah, cut into ½-inch-thick, angled slices

Trader Joe's Everything but the Bagel Sesame Seasoning Blend

maple syrup or Trader Joe's Organic Maple Agave Syrup Blend, to serve (optional)

whipped cream cheese, to serve (optional)

In a wide, shallow bowl, combine the eggs, milk, and 1 tablespoon of sugar and whisk well to combine. In a small bowl, combine the remaining sugar and cinnamon and set aside. Heat a large skillet or frying pan over medium heat. Lightly grease the pan with oil or butter. Dip a slice of the challah in the egg mixture on both sides and place it in the prepared pan. Repeat with additional slices and add them to the pan, allowing for a bit of space between slices. Depending on whether you want to go sweet or savory, sprinkle the uncooked side generously with either some of the cinnamon-sugar mixture or the Everything but the Bagel Sesame Seasoning Blend. Check to see if the bottoms are golden, 2 to 3 minutes, then quickly flip the slices to keep the toppings from falling off. Cook an additional 2 to 3 minutes and remove to a serving plate, seasoned side up. Repeat with the remaining slices. Serve sweet slices with syrup and savory slices with whipped cream cheese.

MAKES: 4 generous servings

VEGAN OPTION: Use ½ cup Trader Joe's Simply Eggless in place of the eggs and replace the milk with a plant-based substitute of your choice. Select one of the other delightful bread choices TJ's offers, like sourdough.

SPICED APRICOT OATS

This is breakfast comfort food to the extreme. Creamy oats are topped with spiced, tangy apricots—perfect for chilly days. Pair with some thick socks and a steaming mug of coffee for ultimate coziness. You can substitute a different kind of dried fruit, like dried plums or peaches as well. Feel free to chop the fruit before cooking. For apple juice, I recommend Trader Joe's Current Crop Gravenstein.

½ to ⅔ cup apple juice

1 cup Trader Joe's Dried Apricots

1 teaspoon ground cinnamon

½ teaspoon Trader Joe's Pumpkin Pie Spice

4 servings Trader Joe's Organic Oats & Flax Instant Oatmeal

2 tablespoons unsalted butter

In a small saucepan over medium heat, add enough apple juice to just cover the apricots. Add the cinnamon and pumpkin pie spice and stir. Simmer the apricots until most of the juice is absorbed and the apricots are tender, 10 to 15 minutes. While the apricots are cooking, make the oats according to the box instructions, enough for 4 servings. Once the oats are done, divide them into 4 bowls. Add ½ tablespoon of butter to each bowl and then divide the apricot mixture among the bowls.

MAKES: 4 servings

VARIATION: Make the oats with apple juice or milk for a richer flavor.

VEGAN OPTION: Replace the butter with Trader Joe's Vegan Buttery Spread.

SAVORY BREAKFAST ROLLS

Imagine a cinnamon roll...but not sweet. Instead picture tender yeasted bread filled with swirls of caramelized onions and cream cheese, and speckled with everything seasoning. The smell will elevate your house to all new levels of deliciousness.

ROLLS:

1 (¼-ounce) packet active dry yeast (about 2¼ teaspoons)

¼ cup warm water

2 tablespoons Trader Joe's Organic Evaporated Cane Juice Sugar

3 tablespoons melted unsalted butter

½ cup warm milk

½ teaspoon salt

4 to 5 cups unbleached all-purpose flour

FILLING:

¼ of 1 (8-ounce) brick cream cheese (2 ounces), at room temperature

1 recipe Caramelized Onion Spread (page 49)

1 egg yolk (for egg wash)

Trader Joe's Everything but the Bagel Sesame Seasoning Blend

To make the rolls: In a large bowl, combine the yeast, warm water, and sugar. Swirl the mixture together and let it sit to proof the yeast. It will become thick and cloudy. Add the butter, milk, and salt, and mix well. Incorporate the flour 1 cup at a time, until a dough comes together. The dough should be tacky. Knead until elastic, about 5 minutes. Place the dough in a lightly oiled bowl. Cover with a kitchen towel and let the dough rise until doubled, about 1 hour.

To make the filling: In the bowl of a stand mixer or in a medium mixing bowl, mix the cream cheese until soft. Add the onion spread and mix until combined. Turn out the dough onto a lightly floured surface and gently knead. Roll out the dough into a 12 x 18-inch rectangle. Spread the cream cheese-onion mixture on the dough to within ½ inch of the edge of the dough. Roll the dough tightly into a log, beginning from the long edge. Cut the dough into 12 even slices and arrange the rolls in an ungreased 9 x 13-inch pan. If baking immediately, cover and let the rolls rise until they are are doubled, about 1 hour. Alternately, if prepping the night before, cover the pan with a tight lid or plastic wrap and refrigerate overnight, allowing the pan to sit out at room temperature for at least 30 minutes before proceeding to the next step.

Whisk the egg yolk with a splash of water and brush the tops of the rolls with the egg wash. Generously sprinkle Everything but the Bagel Sesame Seasoning Blend over the tops of the rolls. Preheat the oven to 375°F. Bake the rolls, uncovered, for 20 to 25 minutes, or until golden. Let them cool slightly before serving.

MAKES: 12 rolls

VEGAN OPTION: Replace the butter with Trader Joe's Vegan Buttery Spread, the filling with a container of Trader Joe's Vegan Caramelized Onion Dip, and the egg yolk with 1 tablespoon of Trader Joe's Simply Eggless.

COOK'S NOTE: If you're going to do both flavors, either designate a side of the pan for sweet or savory or do the sweet first, then the savory. No one likes a fleck of onion in their cinnamon-sugar.

CRANBERRY BANANA OATMEAL MUFFINS

Bananas and cranberries might not be the most expected combination, but it will quickly become a favorite. Sweet and tart, tender but hearty, these are the ultimate breakfast muffin.

1¼ cups all-purpose flour

1¼ cups Trader Joe's Rolled Oats

½ cup Trader Joe's Organic Evaporated Cane Juice Sugar

1 teaspoon baking powder

½ teaspoon baking soda

½ teaspoon salt

½ teaspoon Trader Joe's Organic Ground Cinnamon

2 cups overripe bananas, mashed (about 4)

⅓ cup neutral vegetable oil

1 egg

1 cup fresh or frozen cranberries

Preheat the oven to 350°F and line the cups of a 12-cup muffin tin with muffin liners. In a medium bowl, combine the flour, oats, sugar, baking powder, and baking soda, salt, and cinnamon, and mix to combine. In a large bowl, mash the bananas, add the oil and egg, then mix to combine. Add the dry ingredients in 2 batches, until just combined. The batter should be thick, but if it's dry, add a splash of milk.

Gently incorporate the cranberries, then divide the batter among the prepared muffin cups, filling them to the top. Bake for 20 to 25 minutes, until a toothpick comes out clean and the tops are golden brown—the time will depend on whether your cranberries are fresh or frozen. Let the muffins cool on a rack for 10 minutes, then transfer them from the pan to the cooling rack to cool completely. Store the cooled muffins in a sealed container at room temperature for up to 3 days, or freeze.

MAKES: 12 muffins

COOK'S NOTE: Every year I stock up on fresh cranberries at TJ's over the holidays and pop them in ziplock bags in the freezer. I'm always grateful I did, as dried cranberries have nothing on fresh.

THE ULTIMATE WAFFLE

This waffle will change your idea of breakfast. And waffles. And life. Well, that might be stretching it a little...but only slightly. This waffle combination is crisp, sweet, tangy, and utterly intoxicating. Stock up on supplies; you'll have a line.

1 tablespoon olive oil

4 large eggs

1 (5.64-ounce) box Trader Joe's Authentic Belgian Waffles

⅓ cup crumbled goat cheese, divided

¼ cup Trader Joe's Organic Maple Agave Syrup Blend, divided

1 small avocado, sliced

In a large sauté pan or skillet, heat the oil over medium heat. Cook the eggs over easy, flipping each egg after only 2 to 3 minutes on each side. While cooking the eggs, toast the waffles in a toaster. Place 2 waffles on each plate. Evenly sprinkle the goat cheese over the waffles. Drizzle with the maple-agave syrup and then top each waffle with a cooked egg. Spread several avocado slices on top of each egg.

MAKES: 2 servings

VEGAN OPTION: Omit the cheese and replace the eggs with Tasty Tofu Scramble (page 23).

Bites and Snacks

Whether you need a quick snack or an appetizer to impress someone, this chapter has delicious treats to meet your needs. Prep some appetizers for your party, plan ahead and make afternoon work pick-me-ups, or dress some of these up for a light dinner with a salad on the side.

- SWEET AND SUNNY FLATBREAD
- HOLY MOLE—IT'S NUTS!
- WHITE BEAN BASIL SPREAD
- MUSHROOM PÂTÉ
- JOEY'S CHERRY PIE BARS
- FANTASTIC FRY BREAD
- ROSEMARY CRISPS
- TEXAS TOTCHOS
- HEAVENLY SWEET 'N' SAVORY BITES
- ROASTED EGGPLANT SPREAD
- CARAMELIZED ONION SPREAD
- TANGY VEGAN CHEESE SPREAD
- HERBED GARLIC POLENTA FRIES
- LEMON AIOLI
- CLASSIC ARTICHOKE DIP
- KIDDIE QUESADILLA
- BANGIN' BLACK BEAN DIP
- EVERYTHING SAVORY SHORTBREAD

SWEET AND SUNNY FLATBREAD

This flatbread recipe will win your heart—sweet and juicy corn with cooling mint and bright lemon tang are fantastic together. It's light and bright: perfect for spring or summer. Trader Joe's Garlic Indian Style Flatbread is an excellent base for this flavorful combo.

1 cup Trader Joe's Organic Super Sweet Cut Corn (in the frozen section), thawed

½ cup crumbled goat cheese

1 tablespoon chopped fresh mint

1 teaspoon grated lemon zest

1 teaspoon olive oil

3 pieces flatbread or pita

Preheat the oven to 375°F. In a small bowl, combine the corn, goat cheese, mint, lemon zest, and oil and gently mix to combine. Spread the mixture evenly over the top of the bread. Bake until the edge of the bread is lightly browned and the cheese is golden, 10 to 15 minutes.

MAKES: 6 servings, multiplies easily

VEGAN OPTION: Omit the goat cheese and replace with chopped cashews, and make sure the bread you're using is vegan.

HOLY MOLE—IT'S NUTS!

I love mixed nuts and I love rich, Mexican flavors. These mole-inspired nuts satisfy on many levels and are a unique and handy snack. Trader Joe's carries such an incredible (and affordable) variety of nuts and seeds, you can always change up the recipe depending on what you prefer. Use raw nuts and seeds, if possible. I like a combination of almonds, cashews, and pumpkin seeds. This recipe became a tester favorite, getting devoured even by little kids, although you might want to tone down the cayenne for them. This is a great way to get some healthy fats in their diet.

2 tablespoons Trader Joe's Unsweetened Cocoa Powder

2 tablespoons Trader Joe's Organic Evaporated Cane Juice Sugar

1½ teaspoons ground cinnamon

¼ to ½ teaspoon cayenne pepper

¼ teaspoon sea salt

1 tablespoon vegetable oil

1 tablespoon plus 1 teaspoon Trader Joe's Organic Maple Agave Syrup Blend

2 cups assorted nuts and seeds

VEGAN, GLUTEN-FREE

Preheat the oven to 300°F and line a baking sheet with parchment paper. In a small bowl, combine the cocoa powder, sugar, cinnamon, cayenne, and salt. In a large bowl, whisk together the oil and maple-agave syrup. Add the nuts and seeds and coat with the oil mixture. Sprinkle the dry mixture over the top of the coated nuts and mix until well coated. Spread out into a thin, single layer on the prepared baking sheet. Bake until the nuts are dry, 20 to 25 minutes, stirring halfway through the cooking time. Let the nuts cool completely. Store in an airtight container at room temperature for up to 2 weeks.

MAKES: 8 to 10 servings

WHITE BEAN BASIL SPREAD

This spread is creamy, garlicky, and basily—what more could a person want? Slathered on bread or crackers, it's really the bee's knees.

1 medium head garlic

¼ cup plus 1 tablespoon olive oil, divided

1 (15-ounce) can Trader Joe's White Kidney Beans, drained and rinsed

1 (2.5-ounce) container Trader Joe's Fresh Basil, stems removed

salt and pepper

crackers, bread, and crudités, to serve

VEGAN, GLUTEN-FREE

Heat the oven to 400°F. Cut off the very top of the head of garlic but leave the skin on. The tops of the cloves should be exposed. Drizzle 1 tablespoon of the oil over the exposed cloves and wrap the head in foil, topside up. Roast the garlic in the oven until the cloves are tender when poked with a fork, 30 to 35 minutes. Remove from the oven, and open the foil to let the garlic breathe and cool completely. Peel the cooled, roasted garlic and throw the cloves in the bowl of a food processor or blender. Add the beans and remaining oil and process until creamy, 30 to 60 seconds. Scrape down the walls of the food processor or blender and add the basil, salt, and pepper, pulsing to blend, about another minute, scraping down the walls as needed. Serve with crackers, bread, and crudités. If you'd like to heat the spread, scoop it into a small saucepan and heat over medium low heat, stirring often until heated through.

MAKES: 2 cups of spread

MUSHROOM PÂTÉ

I had two foodie omnivores insist there were assorted animal products in this pâté; they could not fathom that such a complex and delicious spread could be made from things such as mushrooms and walnuts. Sometimes in life, it's good to be wrong. The flavor really develops overnight, so if you can, make this the night before serving.

2 tablespoons olive oil

2 cloves garlic, minced

2 teaspoons whole fresh thyme leaves

¼ teaspoon salt

1½ cups Trader Joe's Sliced Crimini Mushrooms

1 cup Trader Joe's Raw California Walnut Pieces

assorted crackers and crudités, to serve

VEGAN

In a medium pan, heat the oil over medium low heat. Add the garlic and cook until fragrant, about 2 minutes. Add the thyme and salt and cook for about 1 minute. Remove and transfer the contents to the bowl of a food processor. Place the mushrooms in the same pan and cook until dark and the juices release, stirring and adding a little water as needed, about 10 minutes. Transfer to the food processor. Add the walnuts and process until smooth, scraping down the sides as needed. Scoop the pâté into a container with a lid and chill for at least 1 hour before serving with assorted crackers and crudités.

MAKES: 1½ cups of pâté

GLUTEN-FREE OPTION: Serve with vegetables instead of crackers.

JOEY'S CHERRY PIE BARS

Rather than breaking the bank on prepackaged treats like fruit and nut bars, take advantage of the abundance of nuts and dried fruit that Joe's sells—it's a steal—and make your own. The combinations are endless.

1 cup Trader Joe's Dried Pitted Tart Montmorency Cherries

¼ cup pitted Trader Joe's Medjool Dates

1 cup Trader Joe's Raw Whole Cashews

¼ teaspoon vanilla extract

⅛ teaspoon ground cinnamon

sprinkle of salt

¼ cup water

VEGAN, GLUTEN-FREE

Line a 9 x 5-inch loaf pan with waxed paper. In a large heatproof bowl, combine the cherries, dates, and cashews, and soak in hot water for 10 minutes. Drain well and place in the bowl of a food processor. Add the vanilla, cinnamon, and salt, and pulse until the ingredients are well ground into a meal. Add the water, 2 tablespoons at a time, until the mixture comes together like a dough. Press the bar mixture into the bottom of the prepared pan. Cover and refrigerate 30 minutes before removing and slicing into bars.

MAKES: 6 bars

BLUEBERRY MUFFIN VARIATION: Omit the cinnamon and replace the cherries with dried blueberries and the cashews with raw walnuts.

PB & J VARIATION: Use the berry of your choice for the "jelly" and substitute ½ cup of unsalted peanuts for ½ cup of the cashews.

CHOCOLATE BLISS VARIATION: Use the berry of your choice—I love cherries with chocolate—and add 2 tablespoons of Trader Joe's Unsweetened Cocoa Powder and 2 tablespoons chopped semisweet chocolate chips to the mix. You may need an extra tablespoon of water to get them to the right consistency.

FANTASTIC FRY BREAD

Fry bread is pretty self-explanatory; it's bread that is fried. This recipe is a perfect addition to a movie night and is basic enough to whip up for unexpected company. Who doesn't love chewy, lightly crispy breadsticks with yummy dipping sauces? (The correct answer is: nobody.)

1½ to 2 cups mild vegetable oil, for frying

1 (16-ounce) package Trader Joe's Garlic and Herb Pizza Dough (in the refrigerated case), at room temperature

1 (16-ounce) jar Trader Joe's Fat Free Pizza Sauce, to serve (optional)

Besto Pesto (page 119), to serve (optional)

Lemon Aioli (page 50), to serve (optional)

VEGAN

Line a large plate with several paper towels. In a large, shallow pan, heat 1 inch of oil over medium high heat. While the oil is heating, dust a counter and your hands with flour and gently knead the dough. Roll out the dough to about ¼-inch thickness. Cut into strips that will fit in your pan. Check the oil to see if it is ready by dropping in a little piece of dough. If the oil sizzles and the dough quickly turns brown, the oil is ready. Alternatively, check the temperature of the oil with a frying thermometer. You want it to be about 350°F. Please note that hot oil burns (duh), so be careful! Be prepared to move fast. Gently place several strips of dough in the hot oil. The dough should puff up and turn golden quickly, within 2 minutes. Flip the bread to cook the other side, about 1 minute. Using tongs, remove the fry bread strips to drain on the paper-towel-lined plate. Repeat with the remaining dough. Serve the warm fry bread with pizza sauce, pesto, and aioli dipping sauce, if using.

MAKES: 11 to 12 sticks

ROSEMARY CRISPS

I love family-style restaurants, where everyone shares from the same plates and passes them around. It's the communal act of breaking bread in its greatest form. With this rosemary crisp, a large rosemary-infused cracker is left whole, allowing your guests to break off chunks as they like. Pair it with cheese or tapenade; it's lovely with Tangy Vegan Cheese Spread (page 49), White Bean Basil Spread (page 39), or beside a bowl of soup.

2 cups unbleached all-purpose flour

2 tablespoons cold unsalted butter

⅔ cup milk

2 tablespoons minced fresh rosemary leaves

2 teaspoons sea salt

Preheat the oven to 425°F. In the bowl of a food processor, pulse the flour and butter until the mixture becomes coarse and mealy. Add the milk and process until a soft dough comes together. Add the rosemary and mix until incorporated. Flour a clean surface and divide the dough into 4 pieces. Roll out each piece on the surface until it is very thin, about the thickness of a credit card. Carefully transfer each rolled-out piece of dough onto a rimmed baking sheet; you should be able to fit 2 pieces on 1 sheet. It is easiest to do this by rolling the dough onto the rolling pin and then unrolling it on the baking sheet. Sprinkle each sheet of dough with the sea salt. Bake until they are crisp and browned on the edges, 15 to 20 minutes. Let the crisps cool on a cooling rack for 10 minutes before removing them from the baking sheet. Allow to cool completely on a cooling rack.

MAKES: 4 large crisps

VEGAN OPTION: Replace the butter and milk with Trader Joe's Vegan Buttery Spread and nondairy milk.

TEXAS TOTCHOS

Tots and nachos come together in this delicious and slightly messy treat that's sure to be popular with everyone. These totchos are Texas style, smothered in chili. You can always mix it up with toppings: shredded cheese, salsa, pico de gallo, sour cream, guacamole... the options go on and on. If you go a little nuts, though, you might opt for forks over fingers. Just sayin'.

½ (2-pound) bag Trader Joe's Trader Potato Tots

1 (14.7-ounce) can Trader Joe's Organic Vegetarian Chili

1½ cups Trader Joe's Shredded 3 Cheese Blend

Optional toppings: salsa, guacamole, sour cream, cilantro

GLUTEN-FREE

Preheat the oven to 400°F. Spread the tots on an ungreased rimmed baking sheet. Bake until crispy, 18 to 20 minutes. While the tots are cooking, heat the chili in a medium pot over medium heat, stirring often. To assemble, place a layer of tots on a plate. Top with a layer of chili and a sprinkling of cheese. Add the other toppings, if using.

MAKES: 5 to 6 servings

VEGAN OPTION: Replace the cheese with a vegan cheese or omit.

HEAVENLY SWEET 'N' SAVORY BITES

Fresh baguette or pita, topped with juicy pear slices, caramelized onions, and tangy cheese...seriously, these bites are heavenly. If you prep your onion spread ahead of time, you'll be able to make your guests feel spoiled with minimal effort. For the most delicious pears, I suggest using D'Anjou or Bartlett. For the figs, Black Mission or Calimyrna are both wonderful.

1 baguette, sliced on the diagonal into ¾-inch slices (about 15 to 20 total) or 15 to 20 Trader Joe's Mini Pita Pockets

1 to 2 ripe pears, sliced into ¼-inch slices

1 cup Caramelized Onion Spread (page 49)

½ cup crumbled blue cheese

¼ cup chopped figs

Preheat the oven to 350°F. Spread out the baguette slices on a baking sheet. Top each piece of baguette with a slice of pear. Add a healthy tablespoon of the onion spread, then top with a sprinkle of blue cheese and a sprinkle of chopped figs. Bake until the cheese gets melty and the edges of the baguette are crisp, 8 to 10 minutes.

MAKES: 15 to 20 bites

VEGAN OPTION: Replace the blue cheese with a schmear of the Tangy Vegan Cheese Spread (page 49) under the pear slice.

ROASTED EGGPLANT SPREAD

This eggplant spread is easy and quite tasty—I say that as a self-admitted eggplant hater! Everyone will like this, regardless of which side they normally take in the great eggplant debate. Use this as an appetizer with breads and crudités or as a spread on sandwiches.

1 large eggplant

2 tablespoons olive oil

2 cloves garlic, minced

½ cup jarred Trader Joe's Fire-Roasted Red Peppers, chopped

VEGAN, GLUTEN-FREE

Preheat the oven to 400°F and line a rimmed baking sheet with parchment paper. Split the eggplant in half lengthwise and place cut-side down on the prepared baking sheet. Roast the eggplant until very tender, 25 to 35 minutes, depending on the size of the eggplant. Let cool for 20 to 30 minutes before scooping out the flesh. Heat the olive oil in a small sauté pan over medium low heat. Add the garlic and cook until fragrant, about 1 minute. Add the chopped pepper and cook until heated through. In the bowl of a food processor or blender, pulse the garlic mixture with the eggplant mixture until smooth but a little chunky. If necessary, return the mixture to the pot to heat through.

MAKES: 2 cups of spread

CARAMELIZED ONION SPREAD

A good caramelized onion recipe is worth its weight in…well, onions. Nothing smells better than sautéed onions, and the resulting flavor is worth the slow cooking time.

3 tablespoons olive oil

4 large yellow onions, halved and sliced into thin half-moons

sprinkle of salt

1 tablespoon red wine vinegar

1 tablespoon Trader Joe's Organic Maple Agave Syrup Blend

VEGAN, GLUTEN-FREE

In a sauté pan, heat the oil over medium low heat. Add the onions and salt and sauté until translucent, 5 to 7 minutes. Reduce the heat to low, add the vinegar and maple-agave syrup, and continue to cook, covered, stirring often. Cook until the onions are sweet and golden brown, 45 to 60 minutes. It takes awhile, but it's worth the wait. Use the onion spread on crusty bread or in sandwiches. It's also delicious added to tofu scrambles or omelets. Store in covered in the fridge and use within a week of making.

MAKES: 2 cups of spread

TANGY VEGAN CHEESE SPREAD

This versatile spread has only two simple ingredients and easily replaces many different kinds of cheese. It's also a tasty spread on crackers! Of course, it doesn't have to be vegan and can be made with dairy cream cheese as well.

4 ounces Trader Joe's nondairy spread, softened

2 tablespoons Trader Joe's Olive Tapenade with Kalamata & Chalikidiki Olives

VEGAN

In a small bowl, cream together the cream cheese and tapenade until well incorporated and smooth. Store in a covered container in the fridge for up to a week.

MAKES: ½ cup of spread

HERBED GARLIC POLENTA FRIES

Trader Joe's Organic Polenta is gluten-free and oh-so-delicious, so this appetizer is a win for anyone and everyone. Serve with creamy, tangy aioli and you've got bite-size happiness.

1 (18-ounce) log Trader Joe's Organic Polenta

2 tablespoons olive oil

2 teaspoons garlic powder

1 tablespoon dried oregano

½ teaspoon sea salt

⅓ cup Lemon Aioli (recipe follows), to serve

VEGAN, GLUTEN-FREE

Preheat the oven to 400°F and line a baking sheet with parchment paper. Prepare the polenta slices by cutting into ½-inch disks, then strips (about 3 to 4 strips per disk). In a small bowl, whisk the olive oil, garlic powder, and oregano to combine. Gently toss the polenta with the olive oil mixture and spread in an even layer on the prepared baking sheet. Sprinkle with the sea salt. Bake until slightly browned and crispy on the edges, 35 to 40 minutes, flipping halfway through. Serve the fries warm with the aioli.

MAKES: 4 servings

LEMON AIOLI

The reduced-fat mayonnaise at Trader Joe's is (oddly) vegan. Hooray!

1 teaspoon olive oil

2 cloves garlic, minced

1 tablespoon lemon juice

½ teaspoon grated lemon zest

⅓ cup Trader Joe's Reduced Fat Mayonnaise

salt and pepper

VEGAN, GLUTEN-FREE

Heat the olive oil in a small sauté pan or skillet over medium low heat. Sauté the garlic just to remove bitterness, about 1 minute. Remove from the heat to cool. In a small bowl, whisk together the garlic, lemon juice, and lemon zest. Add the mayonnaise and mix until incorporated. Season to taste with salt and pepper. Store in a covered container and refrigerate until ready to use.

MAKES: ⅓ cup of aioli

CLASSIC ARTICHOKE DIP

Overplayed as it may be, artichoke dip continues to be an appetizer menu staple for a reason: It's delicious! This recipe is simple and makes a large quantity, so ready yourself with lots of bread and crudités (a.k.a. artichoke dip delivery devices)!

2 tablespoons olive oil

½ medium yellow onion, diced

2 leeks, whites and light-green parts only, chopped

5 to 6 cloves garlic, minced

4 cups Trader Joe's Organics Baby Spinach

1 (14-ounce) can Trader Joe's Artichoke Hearts, drained and chopped

8 ounces cream cheese

¾ cup Trader Joe's Reduced Fat Mayonnaise

bread, crackers, and vegetables, for dipping

GLUTEN-FREE

Preheat the oven to 350°F. Lightly grease a 9-inch pie pan. In a medium sauté pan or skillet, heat the olive oil over medium heat. Add the onion and leeks and sauté until they start to soften slightly, 3 to 4 minutes. Add the garlic and sauté until the mixture is glistening and fragrant, 2 minutes longer. Add the spinach and cover, letting the spinach steam until wilted, about 2 minutes. Transfer the onion mixture to the bowl of a food processor or blender. Add the artichokes, cream cheese, and mayonnaisennaise, and pulse to combine. Spread the mixture into the prepared pie pan. Bake until the dip is bubbling and browned on the edges, 35 to 40 minutes. Remove and let cool for 10 minutes before serving. Serve with bread, crackers, and vegetables.

MAKES: 10 to 12 servings

VEGAN OPTION: Replace the cream cheese with Trader Joe's nondairy spread.

KIDDIE QUESADILLA

We call it a kiddie quesadilla because, sure, kids like it. But really, you know you're making it for yourself. And that's totally okay, no judgment.

2 ounces cream cheese

2 Trader Joe's Whole Wheat Flour Tortillas

1 to 2 tablespoons Trader Joe's Organic Evaporated Cane Juice Sugar

1 teaspoon ground cinnamon

honey or applesauce, to serve (optional)

Spread 2 tablespoons of the cream cheese on the inside of each the tortilla. Mix the sugar (to your preferred sweetness) and cinnamon together, and sprinkle evenly over the cream cheese. Fold the tortillas in half to make two half-moons. Heat a large, dry sauté pan or skillet over medium heat. Cook 1 tortilla until golden brown, about 2 minutes on each side. The cream cheese center should be a little oozy. Repeat with the other tortilla. Using a pizza cutter, cut into wedges. Eat as is or with a drizzle of honey or applesauce "salsa."

MAKES: 2 servings

....

VEGAN OPTION: Replace the cream cheese with Trader Joe's nondairy spread and the honey with Trader Joe's Organic Blue Agave Sweetener.

....

BANGIN' BLACK BEAN DIP

This simple black bean dip has a complex flavor but it comes together quickly and reheats well, making it great for last-minute get-togethers or potlucks.

1 (15.5-ounce) can Trader Joe's Organic Black Beans

½ (12-ounce) jar Trader Joe's Double Roasted Salsa

½ (4-ounce) can Trader Joe's New Mexico Hatch Valley Fire Roasted Diced Green Chile

1 cup Trader Joe's Shredded 3 Cheese Blend

corn chips, to serve

GLUTEN-FREE

In the bowl of a food processor or blender, combine the black beans, including their liquid, and the salsa and chiles. Pulse until mostly blended but still a little chunky. Transfer to a medium pot over medium heat and cook the mixture until heated through and bubbling, about 5 minutes. Remove from the heat and add the cheese, to melt. Serve with corn chips.

MAKES: 3 cups of dip

VEGAN OPTION: Replace the cheese with a nondairy version or omit.

EVERYTHING SAVORY SHORTBREAD

Crisp and savory, but rather than crunchy like a cracker, these are tender like classic, buttery shortbread. These will likely become a favorite snack and welcome addition to any cheese plate you make.

1 stick (8 tablespoons) unsalted butter, at room temperature

1 cup finely grated Parmesan cheese

¼ teaspoon onion powder

⅛ teaspoon garlic powder

⅛ teaspoon salt

crack of fresh pepper

1¼ cups all-purpose flour

1 egg

Trader Joe's Everything but the Bagel Sesame Seasoning Blend

In a large bowl, use a hand mixer to mix the butter until creamy. Add the cheese, onion powder, garlic powder, salt, and pepper. Mix to combine. Add the flour in 2 batches until just combined. The dough may be a little crumbly but should hold together if pressed (the texture of Play-Doh). If needed, add water 1 teaspoon at a time. Shape the dough into a 2-inch diameter log and wrap in plastic wrap. Refrigerate for at least 1 hour. Preheat the oven to 350°F. On a baking sheet lined with parchment paper, cut out dough into ⅜-inch circles and place 1 inch apart on the baking sheet. In a small bowl, whisk the egg and brush the tops of the cookies. Sprinkle liberally with Everything but the Bagel Sesame Seasoning Blend. Bake for 18 to 20 minutes, rotating the sheet once halfway through, until shortbread edges are set, but before they turn golden.

MAKES: 2½ dozen cookies

COOK'S NOTE: Parmesan is perfect in these but you can always opt for a different hard cheese, such as Romano, which has a more pronounced flavor.

Salads

Salads run the gamut from bowls filled with lettuce and vegetables to delicious pastas made for picnics and summer potlucks. On a hot day, they also stand in for light suppers—so refreshing.

- STRAWBERRY-BASIL SALAD
- STRAWBERRY-BASIL VINAIGRETTE
- THREE-BEAN SALAD
- QUICK PICKLED ONIONS
- SLAWVOCADO SALAD
- FAST LENTIL SALAD
- ALL-PURPOSE VINAIGRETTE
- POTLUCK PASTA SALAD
- SPRINGY ASPARAGUS RICE SALAD
- CUMIN CITRUS SALAD
- MASSAGED SPINACH SALAD
- GODDESS CONFETTI SALAD
- GREEK CHICKPEA-LAF
- SIMPLE FRUIT SALAD
- BUTTERNUT SQUASH PILAF
- GOAT CHEESE, BEET, AND GOLDEN BERRY PILAF
- EASY POTATO SALAD

STRAWBERRY-BASIL SALAD

The combination of strawberries and basil is truly out of this world. Sweet and savory come together in a fragrant salad that will certainly catch the attention of your guests.

1 (5-ounce) package Trader Joe's Organics Baby Romaine

1 (2.5-ounce) container Trader Joe's Fresh Basil, leaves removed from the stems

1 cup fresh strawberries, sliced

1 cup Trader Joe's Persian Cucumbers, sliced into ¼-inch coins

⅓ cup Strawberry-Basil Vinaigrette (recipe follows)

⅓ cup crumbled goat cheese

GLUTEN-FREE

Place the romaine lettuce in a large bowl along with the basil leaves. Add the strawberries and cucumbers and then toss with the vinaigrette. Top the salad with the goat cheese.

MAKES: 3 to 4 servings

VEGAN OPTION: Omit the goat cheese.

STRAWBERRY-BASIL VINAIGRETTE

Basil makes this vinaigrette especially fragrant, and the sweetness of the strawberries really takes it into sublime territory. For extra basil intensity, add some fresh basil leaves to your lettuce mix.

½ cup chopped fresh strawberries

¼ cup mild white vinegar

¼ cup olive oil

¼ cup fresh basil leaves

VEGAN, GLUTEN-FREE

Combine the strawberries, vinegar, olive oil, and basil in the bowl of a food processor and blend until emulsified and the strawberries are incorporated. Use within 2 days of making.

MAKES: 1 to 1¼ cups of vinaigrette

THREE-BEAN SALAD

This salad is full of flavor and it tastes delicious both cold and warm with unique seasoning.

1 (15-ounce) can Trader Joe's Organic Pinto Beans, drained and rinsed

1 (15-ounce) can Trader Joe's Organic Black Beans, drained and rinsed

1 (15-ounce) can Trader Joe's Organic Garbanzo Beans, drained and rinsed

¼ cup olive oil

2 teaspoons fresh thyme

1 teaspoon garlic powder

¼ cup fresh lime juice

½ pint Quick Pickled Onions (recipe below), to serve

VEGAN, GLUTEN-FREE

Place all of the beans in a large bowl or container. Heat the olive oil in a small pan over medium heat. Add the thyme and garlic powder. Cook until fragrant, about 1 minute. Remove from the heat and add the lime juice. Whisk to combine. Pour the olive oil mixture over the beans and toss to combine. Refrigerate, covered, and let the sauce infuse the beans for at least 2 hours. To serve, toss again with any settled liquid and top with some of the pickled onions.

MAKES: 4 to 6 servings

QUICK PICKLED ONIONS

These onions go wonderfully over salads or on sandwiches, or they're delicious eaten right out of the jar! They last in the fridge up to three weeks.

¾ cup white vinegar

3 tablespoons Trader Joe's Organic Evaporated Cane Juice Sugar

⅛ teaspoon salt

1 large red onion, cut into thin rounds

VEGAN, GLUTEN-FREE

In a small pot over medium high heat, bring the vinegar, sugar, and salt to a simmer. Whisk until the sugar is dissolved. Lower heat to medium low, add the onion, and mix to coat the onions with the mixture and to wilt them. Cook for 2 to 3 minutes, then remove from the heat. Let the mixture cool completely before transferring to a heatproof container. Refrigerate, covered, for at least 2 hours before serving.

MAKES: 1 (½-pint) jar

SLAWVOCADO SALAD

This flavorful play on coleslaw is full of healthy fat and delicious, creamy flavor.

1 tablespoon olive oil

1 clove garlic, minced

2 large avocados

¼ cup chopped cilantro, plus extra for garnish

juice of 1 small lime

sprinkle of salt

¼ to ⅓ cup water

1 (12-ounce) bag Trader Joe's Organic Broccoli Slaw

2 Roma tomatoes, cored and chopped

½ jalapeño pepper, diced (optional)

VEGAN, GLUTEN-FREE

In the bowl of a food processor, combine the olive oil, garlic, and avocados. Pulse until smooth, scraping down the sides of the bowl as needed. Add the cilantro, lime juice, and salt. Add enough water to make the avocado sauce the consistency of a creamy dressing. In a large bowl, toss the avocado dressing with the broccoli slaw. Top with the tomatoes, jalapeño, if using, and garnish with cilantro.

MAKES: 6 to 8 servings

FAST LENTIL SALAD

I like salads that are light and fresh, but stick to your ribs, and this one certainly qualifies. Baby greens and lentils make up the base, while the salad is rounded out with crunchy peppers, goat cheese, and a tangy vinaigrette.

1 (5-ounce) bag Trader Joe's Organics Baby Spring Mix

1½ cups Trader Joe's Steamed Lentils (in the refrigerated case), rinsed

1 cup Trader Joe's Super Sweet Baby Bell Peppers, sliced and seeds diskarded

¼ red onion, sliced into thin half-moons

¼ to ⅓ cup All-Purpose Vinaigrette (page 65)

⅓ cup crumbled goat cheese

¼ recipe Quick Pickled Onions (page 60) (optional)

GLUTEN-FREE

In a large bowl, place the lettuce, lentils, bell peppers, and red onion. Toss with the vinaigrette. Top with the goat cheese and, if using, the pickled onions.

MAKES: 3 to 4 generous servings

VEGAN OPTION: Omit the goat cheese.

COOK'S NOTE: You'll have enough leftover lentils to make the Thai Lentil Simmer (page 87)!

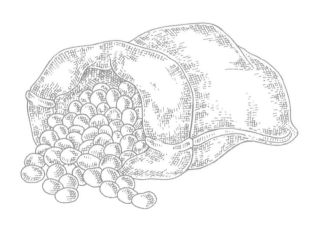

ALL-PURPOSE VINAIGRETTE

I use this mellow vinaigrette on everything, no joke. Obviously, it's great on salads, but I toss steamed vegetables in it, or drizzle it over tofu or potatoes. It's the simple things in life that are the best.

⅓ cup Trader Joe's White Balsamic Vinegar

¼ cup extra-virgin olive oil

2 cloves garlic, minced

1 teaspoon dried basil

VEGAN, GLUTEN-FREE

Whisk the vinegar, olive oil, garlic, and basil together until blended. (I like to pour them into a mason jar and shake them up.) Refrigerate, covered, for up to 2 weeks. Note that olive oil can harden when refrigerated, so it might need to sit out for a few minutes before using.

MAKES: ⅔ cup of vinaigrette

POTLUCK PASTA SALAD

This pasta salad is an updated classic: Corkscrew fusilli catches tasty Italian dressing in its coils, mingling with an assortment of vegetables and a tasty topping of feta. Using the brown rice pasta also makes this dish gluten-free!

2½ cups Trader Joe's Organic Brown Rice Fusilli Pasta

⅓ to ½ cup Trader Joe's Tuscan Italian Dressing

1 medium red or orange bell pepper, diced

1 cup halved cherry tomatoes

1 cup sliced mushrooms

¼ to ½ cup crumbled feta cheese

GLUTEN-FREE

Cook the pasta according to the package directions. Drain the pasta and rinse with cool water. In a large bowl, toss the pasta with the dressing, then add the prepared vegetables. Add additional dressing, if desired. Top with feta. Serve immediately, or refrigerate and serve cold.

MAKES: 6 to 8 servings

VEGAN OPTION: Omit the feta.

SPRINGY ASPARAGUS RICE SALAD

This pilaf is spring in its purest and simplest edible form: fresh, crisp asparagus, tender rice, with a little bit of tang. Eaten warm or cold, it's delicious.

4 tablespoons olive oil, divided

½ medium yellow or white onion, diced

2 cloves garlic, minced

1 pound fresh, thin asparagus, cut into 1-inch pieces

3 tablespoons rice vinegar

2 (30-ounce) boxes Trader Joe's Rice Medley (in the frozen section), cooked

¼ to ½ cup grated Parmesan cheese

In a large sauté pan or skillet, heat 1 tablespoon of the olive oil over medium low heat. Add the onion and cook until slightly tender, about 2 minutes. Add the garlic and the asparagus and sauté until fragrant. A fork should be able to easily pierce the asparagus, but it should still be crispy. Remove from the heat. Whisk in the remaining olive oil and the vinegar. Toss with the rice and top with Parmesan. Serve warm, or chill and serve cold.

MAKES: 4 to 6 servings

VEGAN OPTION: Omit the cheese.

GLUTEN-FREE OPTION: Most TJ's frozen rice varieties are gluten-free.

CUMIN CITRUS SALAD

This salad is refreshing and unique, yet marries familiar flavors; it's the perfect melding of old and new. Traditional cilantro and cumin come together with crisp cabbage and orange segments to make something crisp, fragrant, and crave-worthy.

1 (10-ounce) bag Trader Joe's Shredded Green Cabbage

2 oranges, segmented

⅓ cup fresh cilantro, packed

2 tablespoons fresh orange juice

2 tablespoons olive oil

¾ teaspoon ground cumin

¼ teaspoon sea salt

1 fresh avocado, sliced

VEGAN, GLUTEN-FREE

Place the shredded cabbage in a large bowl. Segment the orange by using a sharp knife to cut off the peel, including the white pith, from the exterior of the whole orange. Then cut into segments and diskard the membrane. Add the orange segments and the cilantro to the bowl. In a small bowl, whisk together the orange juice, olive oil, cumin, and sea salt. Toss the dressing with the salad. Top with the avocado slices.

MAKES: 4 to 6 servings

MASSAGED SPINACH SALAD

This salad is so simple and perfectly satisfying on a warm day. What more could you want in the middle of summer than some juicy tomatoes, tangy lemon, mellow olive oil, and a hint of sea salt?

4 to 5 cups Trader Joe's Organics
Baby Spinach

2 tablespoons lemon juice

2 to 3 tablespoons olive oil

1 large beefsteak or heirloom
tomato, sliced

sprinkle Trader Joe's Himalayan
Pink Sea Salt

VEGAN, GLUTEN-FREE

Place the spinach in a large bowl. In a small bowl, whisk together the lemon juice and olive oil. Drizzle the mixture over the spinach and, with very clean hands, gently massage it into the leaves, mixing well to coat. Place the spinach on 2 plates and top with slices of tomato. Finish with a light sprinkling of sea salt.

MAKES: 2 salads, multiplies easily

GODDESS CONFETTI SALAD

All hail Trader Joe's Goddess Dressing! That tangy, creamy blessing has perked up many a salad, and here it unifies our vegetables into tasty, tasty harmony.

1 medium cucumber, cubed

1 (8-ounce) container cherry
tomatoes, halved

⅓ cup Trader Joe's Organic
Super Sweet Cut Corn (in the
frozen section), thawed

¼ to ⅓ cup Trader Joe's Goddess
Dressing

baby lettuce greens, to serve

1 ripe avocado, sliced, to serve

VEGAN

In a large bowl, place the cucumber, tomatoes, and corn. Toss with the dressing until coated. Serve on a bed of baby lettuce, topped with avocado slices.

MAKES: 4 servings

GREEK CHICKPEA-LAF

This pilaf is delicious warm or cold and it gets better with age. If you can make it the day before serving, reserve the parsley until just before serving.

1¾ cups water

1¼ cups Trader Joe's Harvest Grains Blend

¼ cup olive oil, divided

½ medium red onion, diced

2 cloves garlic

2 tablespoons dried oregano

¼ teaspoon salt

1 (15-ounce) can Trader Joe's Organic Garbanzo Beans, drained and rinsed

3 Roma tomatoes, cored and diced

¼ cup lemon juice

½ cup feta cheese (optional)

½ cup chopped fresh parsley

In a medium pot over high heat, boil the water and then add the grain blend. Reduce the heat to medium low and simmer with the lid on until the water is absorbed, 15 to 20 minutes. Let the grains cool. In a large sauté pan or skillet over medium low heat, heat 2 tablespoons of the olive oil. Add the red onion and garlic and cook just to heat through and remove the bitterness, 2 to 3 minutes. Add the oregano and salt and stir to combine. Remove from the heat. Add the grains, the remaining 2 tablespoons oil, and the beans, tomatoes, and lemon juice to the sauté pan or skillet and stir to combine. Top with the feta, if using, and parsley just before serving.

MAKES: 6 to 8 servings as a side, 4 as a main dish

VEGAN OPTION: Omit the feta.

COOK'S NOTE: The Harvest Grains Blend is carried seasonally only at some stores, so feel free to substitute an equal amount of quinoa or Israeli couscous if need be.

SIMPLE FRUIT SALAD

This fruit salad comes together quickly and is flexible enough to make with whatever fruit you have on hand. However, I'm partial to the sweetness of the mandarins, the creaminess of the bananas, and the zing of lime juice, all topped with the pomegranate's tang and texture. It's simple with good reason—nature's candy doesn't need much dressing up.

1 (11-ounce) can Trader Joe's Mandarin Oranges

2 bananas, sliced into ¼-inch coins

juice of ½ lime

¼ cup pomegranate seeds

VEGAN, GLUTEN-FREE

In a medium bowl, combine the orange and banana slices. Toss with the lime juice. Serve, topped with pomegranate seeds.

SERVES: 4 side salads

BUTTERNUT SQUASH PILAF

Tangy pickled onions tossed with sweet and earthy squash cubes, nutty farro, spicy arugula, and bits of fragrant Romano cheese—this pilaf is a perfect main dish or delightful side.

1 (12-ounce) bag Trader Joe's Cut Butternut Squash

4 tablespoons olive oil, divided

salt and pepper

1 cup Trader Joe's 10 Minute Farro

2 to 3 tablespoons red wine vinegar

½ teaspoon salt

½ teaspoon Trader Joe's Organic Evaporated Cane Juice Sugar

½ cup red onion, finely chopped

½ bag Trader Joe's Wild Arugula

½ cup Trader Joe's Asiago Cheese, finely shredded

GLUTEN-FREE

Preheat the oven to 375°F. In a large bowl, add the butternut squash and toss with 2 tablespoons of the olive oil. Season generously with salt and pepper. Spread out the squash on a baking sheet. Roast until tender, about 20 to 30 minutes, tossing occasionally. While the squash is roasting, prepare the farro according to the simmer instructions on the package. Next, prep the dressing. In a bowl, combine the remaining olive oil, red wine vinegar (to your preferred taste), salt, and sugar, and whisk. Add the onion and mix to coat. Set aside. Once the squash is done, allow it to partially cool. In a large bowl, combine the squash, farro, and onion dressing mixture. Toss to coat. Taste and adjust seasonings accordingly. While the mixture is still warm, toss it with the arugula, allowing it to wilt slightly before adding the cheese. Serve warm or cold.

GOAT CHEESE, BEET, AND GOLDEN BERRY PILAF

Gooseberries, golden berries, ground cherries…whatever you call them, their mild sweetness and firm flesh are a perfect complement to the sweet, earthy beets and sweet, creamy goat cheese. Thankfully, Trader Joe's sells them by the clamshell, if you can reserve any from immediate consumption. The combination is intoxicating.

1½ cups Trader Joe's 10 Minute Farro

2 tablespoons olive oil

3 tablespoons Trader Joe's Balsamic Vinegar of Modena

1 teaspoon Dijon mustard

salt and pepper

1 (8-ounce) container Trader Joe's Steamed and Peeled Baby Beets, quartered

1 (4-ounce) log Trader Joe's Chevre with Honey Goat's Milk Cheese, crumbled

1 cup Trader Joe's Sun Belle Golden Berries, quartered

GLUTEN-FREE

In a pot, prepare the farro according to the simmer instructions on the package. In a small bowl, combine the olive oil, balsamic vinegar, mustard, and salt and pepper to make a vinaigrette. Whisk and adjust the flavor to taste. Once the farro is done, allow it to cool for about 10 minutes, then fluff and transfer to a large bowl. Add the beets and the vinaigrette and toss to coat. Add the crumbled goat cheese and mix, allowing some of it to melt, while also leaving little pockets of cheesy goodness. Add the golden berries last. Top with additional pepper to taste. Serve as a side, warm or cold, or warm over a bed of fresh spinach leaves.

MAKES: 4 large servings

EASY POTATO SALAD

This German-esque potato salad is very quick, and it showcases TJ's amazing whole grain Dijon mustard. Everyone will want to know your secret ingredient.

2 pounds yellow or red potatoes, diced into 1-inch cubes

1 tablespoon olive oil

½ small yellow or white onion, diced

¼ cup Trader Joe's Organic Unfiltered Apple Cider Vinegar

2 tablespoons Trader Joe's Organic Evaporated Cane Juice Sugar

1 tablespoon Dijon mustard

½ cup coarsely chopped green onions

salt and pepper

VEGAN, GLUTEN-FREE

Place the potatoes in a large pot and cover with enough water to submerge. Simmer over medium high heat until tender, about 15 minutes. Drain and transfer to a large bowl. In a small pot, heat the oil over low heat and sauté the onions, just to warm, 1 to 2 minutes. Remove the pot from the heat and add the vinegar, sugar, and mustard. Whisk to dissolve the sugar. Pour the vinegar mixture over the potatoes and gently toss. Season to taste with salt and pepper, cover, and refrigerate to cool. Top with the green onions before serving

MAKES: 8 to 10 side salads

Soups and Stews

Oh yeah, baby. Thick and hearty stews, creamy and tasty soups—nothing can replace these guys on cold days or when you're feeling under the weather.

- HERBED VEGETABLE STEW
- HEARTY BEAN STEW
- MY ROCKIN' CHICKPEA SOUP
- MIGHTY MINESTRONE
- TUSCAN TOMATO SOUP
- GARLICKY GREEN SOUP
- MEATY MUSHROOM STEW
- QUICK MEXICAN STEW
- QUICKY CHICKPEA SOUP
- THAI LENTIL SIMMER
- ROASTED CORN CHOWDER
- SOUPER EASY MUSHROOM SOUP
- AFRICAN PEANUT STEW
- THREE-BEAN CHILI
- CREAMY GNOCCHI DUMPLING SOUP

HERBED VEGETABLE STEW

This stew is pretty straightforward. No game-playing, no bait and switch. Just straight-up, thick, chunky stew infused with fresh herbs. This would be a great recipe to pair with Vegan Biscuits (page 159) or a side of Sesame Kale (page 119).

2 tablespoons olive oil

1 large white or yellow onion, diced

3 cloves garlic, thinly sliced

2 medium russet potatoes, peeled and cut into 1-inch cubes

1 sweet potato, peeled and cut into 1-inch cubes

1 (15-ounce) can Trader Joe's Organic Kidney Beans, drained and rinsed

1 (14.5-ounce) can Trader Joe's Organic Tomatoes Diced & No Salt Added

1 cup fresh green beans, ends trimmed and cut into 1-inch pieces

1 large zucchini, cut into ½-inch-thick half-moons

1½ cups water

2 tablespoons unbleached all-purpose flour

2 tablespoons chopped fresh oregano

2 tablespoons chopped fresh thyme

2 tablespoons chopped fresh rosemary

½ teaspoon salt

pepper

VEGAN

Heat the olive oil in a large stockpot over medium high heat. Add the onion and sauté until translucent, about 5 minutes. Add the garlic slices and cook for about 1 minute. Add the potatoes, sweet potato, beans, and tomatoes (including their juices) and just enough water to cover the bottom of the pot. Cover with a lid, reduce the heat to medium low, and simmer until the potatoes are slightly softened, 15 to 20 minutes, stirring often. If needed, add a little more water during that time. Add the green beans and zucchini. In a small bowl, whisk together the water and flour. Add the oregano, thyme, and rosemary, and pour the mixture into the stockpot. Add the salt and a little pepper and bring to a boil, stirring often. Once the stew boils, reduce the heat to low and simmer until the sauce is thickened and the vegetables are tender, about 10 minutes.

MAKES: 4 to 5 servings

GLUTEN-FREE OPTION: Replace the flour with a gluten-free flour or cornstarch.

HEARTY BEAN STEW

This stew is one of those perfect set-it-and-forget-it types. Let it simmer away while you clean house, cook other things, or park yourself on the couch for a mini TV marathon. The next thing you know, dinner is served.

2 tablespoons olive oil

1 small yellow or white onion, chopped

2 to 3 cloves garlic, minced

1 (14.5-ounce) can Trader Joe's Organic Tomatoes Diced & No Salt Added

1 small potato, peeled and diced

1 carrot, peeled and cut into half-moons

1 small red or orange bell pepper, cored and chopped

1 cup Trader Joe's 17 Bean & Barley Mix

3 cups water

1 large zucchini, cut into half-moons

2 cups spinach or kale

VEGAN

In a large stockpot, heat the oil over medium heat. Add the onion and cook until it begins to soften, about 5 minutes. Add the garlic and cook until the onions are translucent and the garlic is fragrant, about 2 minutes longer. Add the tomatoes, potato, carrot, and bell pepper. Bring to a simmer, stirring often. Add the bean and barley mix and water and reduce the heat to medium low. Cover the pot with a lid and simmer the stew, stirring occasionally, until the beans are tender, 1½ to 2 hours. Add the zucchini and kale and cook until the zucchini is tender, 10 minutes longer.

MAKES: 6 to 8 servings

MY ROCKIN' CHICKPEA SOUP

This stew is a little spicy and a little sweet, and it's topped with Trader Joe's perfect figs. The essence of Morocco in a matter of minutes.

2 tablespoons olive oil

1 small yellow or white onion, diced

1½ teaspoons ground cumin

¼ to ½ teaspoon cayenne pepper

2 (15-ounce) cans Trader Joe's Organic Garbanzo Beans, drained and rinsed

1 (14.5-ounce) can Trader Joe's Organic Tomatoes Diced & No Salt Added

1 cup Trader Joe's Israeli Couscous, cooked

2 tablespoons to ¼ cup water

3 tablespoons Trader Joe's Organic Thompson Seedless Raisins

¼ cup chopped Trader Joe's Black Mission Figs

sour cream, to serve

chopped fresh cilantro, for garnish

In a large stockpot over medium low heat, heat the oil. Add the onion and cook until translucent, about 5 minutes. Add the cumin and cayenne and cook until fragrant, about 1 minute. Add the beans and tomatoes, (including their juices) and bring to a simmer. While the beans are simmering, prepare the couscous according to the package directions. Add enough water to bring the mixture to a stew-like consistency. Add the raisins and cook until heated through and plumped, about 5 minutes. Serve the stew over the couscous, and top with figs, sour cream, and cilantro.

MAKES: 4 to 5 servings

VEGAN OPTION: Omit the sour cream or substitute with a nondairy equivalent.

MIGHTY MINESTRONE

This is a total comfort soup and is as healthy as it is hearty. You can always mix up the vegetables and use what you have available. Potatoes, green beans, peas, parsnips, squash—there are a million options!

1 tablespoon olive oil

1 small white or yellow onion, chopped

3 cloves garlic, minced

2 medium carrots, chopped

2 stalks celery, chopped

2 teaspoons dried oregano

1 teaspoon dried thyme

6 cups Trader Joe's Organic Hearty Vegetable Broth

1 (15-ounce) can Trader Joe's Organic Kidney Beans, drained and rinsed

1 cup Trader Joe's Italian Orzo

1 (14.5-ounce) can Trader Joe's Organic Tomatoes Diced & No Salt Added

2 cups Trader Joe's Kale, chopped

warm bread, to serve

VEGAN

In a large stockpot over medium heat, heat the olive oil and sauté the onion for about 2 minutes. Add the garlic and continue cooking until the onion is translucent, 3 to 5 more minutes. Incorporate the carrots and celery and sauté for about 5 minutes, stirring often. Add the oregano and thyme and cook, stirring, until fragrant, about 1 minute. Add the vegetable broth, stirring to combine, and increase the heat to medium high, bringing to a boil. Add the beans and orzo and reduce the heat to medium. Let the soup simmer, covered, until the beans and grain are tender, about 30 minutes. Add the tomatoes, including their juices, and cook through, about 10 minutes. Remove the soup from the heat and add the chopped kale. Stir to combine and wilt the greens, and let sit for about 5 minutes before serving. Serve the soup with warm, crusty bread.

MAKES: 5 to 6 hearty servings

TUSCAN TOMATO SOUP

This soup blends creamy tomatoes and hearty potatoes into a rich broth. The unconventional pairing of flavors will quickly become one of your favorites.

2 medium yellow or red potatoes, peeled and chopped

1 (14.5-ounce) can Trader Joe's Organic Tomatoes Diced & No Salt Added

2 tablespoons olive oil

1 small yellow or white onion, diced

2 cloves garlic, minced

2 cups sliced celery

1 (15-ounce) can Trader Joe's Organic Kidney Beans, drained and rinsed

1 teaspoon dried oregano

¼ teaspoon salt

1½ to 2 cups water

VEGAN, GLUTEN-FREE

In a small stockpot, cover the potatoes with just enough water to submerge, and simmer over medium heat until tender, 10 to 15 minutes. Drain the water and transfer the potatoes to a blender or food processor and blend with the tomatoes. Set aside. In the stockpot, heat the oil over medium heat and sauté the onion until it starts to slightly soften, about 3 minutes. Add the garlic and sauté for 2 more minutes. Add the celery, beans, oregano, and salt, and mix to combine. Add the potato mixture to the pot and simmer, with the lid on, until the celery is tender, 15 to 20 minutes. Add the water until the soup is the consistency you'd like. Cook until heated through, 5 minutes more.

MAKES: 4 to 6 servings

GARLICKY GREEN SOUP

A refreshing and naturally green soup, chock-full of roasted garlic, white beans, and greens, this is sure to help detox and nourish. This recipe is so simple, thick, and delicious. If you like roasted garlic, you'll love this soup.

1 medium to large head garlic

1 tablespoon olive oil, divided

1 (15-ounce) can Trader Joe's White Kidney Beans, drained and rinsed

2 cups Trader Joe's Organic Hearty Vegetable Broth

3 cups chopped Trader Joe's Kale, packed

2 cups Trader Joe's Organics Baby Spinach, packed

VEGAN, GLUTEN-FREE

Preheat the oven to 400°F. Chop off the very top of the garlic head and drizzle with 1 teaspoon of the olive oil. Wrap in foil and bake until tender when pierced with a fork, 35 to 40 minutes. Unwrap and let cool for about 20 minutes, and then peel the cloves. In a large stockpot, heat the remaining 2 teaspoons olive oil over medium heat. Add the garlic and cook for 2 minutes, stirring often. Add the beans, 1½ cups of the vegetable broth, and cook until heated through, 8 to 10 minutes. Add the kale and spinach and cover with a lid. Cook until just wilted, about 2 minutes. Blend the soup using an immersion blender or countertop blender. Add the remaining broth, if desired, to achieve preferred consistency.

MAKES: 4 servings

MEATY MUSHROOM STEW

This stew is thick and hearty, and it's infused with herbs and a rich sauce. Trader Joe's has great prices on a variety of mushrooms. This recipe is extra delicious when prepared with crimini, shiitake, or portobellos. For large mushrooms like portobellos, be sure to remove the stems before cooking. Serve the stew over your favorite grain.

2 tablespoons olive oil

1½ pounds mushrooms, chopped

1 small white or yellow onion, diced

3 cloves garlic, minced

2 teaspoons dried thyme

1 teaspoon dried oregano

¼ teaspoon salt

1 large potato, peeled and diced into ½-inch cubes

2 tablespoons Trader Joe's Reduced Sodium Soy Sauce

2 tablespoons red wine vinegar

¾ cup water

2 tablespoons unbleached all-purpose flour

cooked quinoa or rice, to serve

VEGAN

In a large sauté pan or skillet, heat the oil over medium heat. Add the mushrooms and sauté until the juices are released and the mushrooms are tender. Remove the mushrooms to a separate bowl. Add the onion and sauté until translucent, about 3 minutes. Add the garlic, thyme, oregano, and salt and cook until fragrant, about 1 minute. Add the mushrooms back to the pan along with the potatoes. Reduce the heat to low and cover. In a small bowl, whisk together the soy sauce, vinegar, water, and flour. Add the sauce mixture to the pan and bring to a simmer. Cover and let it cook until the sauce thickens and the potatoes are tender, about 15 minutes. Serve over a grain like quinoa or rice.

MAKES: 4 servings

QUICK MEXICAN STEW

This black bean stew is the result of just tossing together a couple of cans of beans and salsa into a pot and letting them simmer. But it has such a complex and flavorful taste that your guests will never believe it was that simple, as they shovel spoonfuls of it into their eager mouths. Quinoa and brown rice are both great options for grain.

2 cups prepared grain

1 tablespoon olive oil

2 bell peppers, sliced into half-strips

2 (15-ounce) cans Trader Joe's Organic Black Beans, drained and rinsed

1 (13.75-ounce) jar Trader Joe's Corn and Chile Tomato-less Salsa

1 ripe avocado, sliced

Optional toppings: sour cream, salsa, crushed tortilla chips

VEGAN

Prepare the grain according to the package directions. Heat the olive oil in a large pot over medium low heat. Sauté the bell peppers until fragrant and slightly softened, about 5 minutes. Add the beans and corn salsa and mix to combine. Cook over medium heat until heated through, about 10 minutes. Divide the grain evenly into 4 bowls and top with the black bean stew. Serve with sliced avocado and toppings of your choice.

MAKES: 4 servings

QUICKY CHICKPEA SOUP

This stew comes together very quickly and is versatile—you can mix up the vegetables you use in order to incorporate your favorites or to clean out your crisper.

2 tablespoons olive oil

1 medium white or yellow onion, diced

2 cloves garlic, minced

2 (15-ounce) cans Trader Joe's Organic Garbanzo Beans, drained and rinsed

1 (28-ounce) can Trader Joe's Organic Tomatoes Diced in Tomato Juice

1 large zucchini, cut into ¼-inch-thick coins, then halved

2 teaspoons capers, drained

salt and pepper

cooked rice, to serve (optional)

VEGAN, GLUTEN-FREE

In a small stockpot, heat the oil over medium heat. Add the onion and sauté until translucent, about 5 minutes. Add the garlic and cook until fragrant, about 1 minute. Add the garbanzos and the tomatoes (including juices) and bring to a simmer. Let the stew cook until the garbanzos are tender and have absorbed some of the tomato juice, about 15 minutes. Add the zucchini and the capers and reduce the heat to low. Cover with a lid and let cook, stirring occasionally, until the zucchini is tender, about 5 more minutes. Season to taste with salt and pepper. Serve alone or over rice, if using.

MAKES: 5 to 6 servings

THAI LENTIL SIMMER

Low on time? This recipe requires very little. So little, in fact, the directions quote the famous infomercial: just set it and forget it. (But do remember to stir!) Also, the TJ's frozen basmati rice is a perfect grain for this.

2 tablespoons olive oil

1 small yellow or white onion, diced

1 medium potato, peeled and cut into ½-inch cubes

½ (17.6-ounce) package Trader Joe's Steamed Lentils

1 (12-ounce) jar Trader Joe's Thai Green Curry Simmer Sauce

2 cups cooked grain

2 large tomatoes, diced and seeded

VEGAN

Heat the oil in a large skillet over medium heat. Add the onions and cook until translucent, about 5 minutes. Add the potato, lentils, and simmer sauce, and reduce the heat to medium low. Cover and let simmer, stirring often, until the potatoes are softened, about 15 minutes. While the potato-lentil mixture is simmering, prepare the grain. Add the tomatoes to the skillet and cook until they are tender, about 5 minutes. Divide the grains among 4 bowls or plates and divide the lentil simmer over the top.

MAKES: 4 servings

GLUTEN-FREE OPTION: Most of the TJ's frozen rice is gluten-free.

ROASTED CORN CHOWDER

This chowder comes together quickly and is comfort food at its very best.

2 tablespoons unsalted butter

1 medium yellow onion, diced

¼ cup all-purpose flour

2 cloves garlic, minced

1 (16-ounce) bag frozen Trader Joe's Roasted Corn

5 cups Trader Joe's Organic Hearty Vegetable Broth

2 large carrots, peeled and chopped in ½-inch-thick half moons

3 medium Yukon Gold potatoes (about 2 cups), peeled and diced to ¾-inch cubes

¼ teaspoon smoked paprika

½ cup milk

salt and pepper

In a large pot, melt the butter and sauté the onion until translucent, about 5 minutes. Sprinkle the flour over the onions and mix to coat, cooking until toasted and golden. Add the garlic and mix until fragrant, about 1 minute. Add the corn, vegetable broth, carrots, potatoes, and smoked paprika. Bring to a simmer and cover, cooking until the potatoes are tender, about 20 minutes. Puree ¼ of the soup in a blender before returning to the pot. Add the milk and mix to combine. Adjust to taste with salt and pepper.

MAKES: 4 servings

SOUPER EASY MUSHROOM SOUP

This recipe is an ode to one of my favorite shows—Party Down. It's HYSTERICAL. This soup recipe is dedicated to the most endearing and pathetic character on the show, Ron, played by the ever-brilliant Ken Marino. His only dream in life is to run a Souper Crackers restaurant. Serve this soup with, of course, crackers. For an extra-rich flavor, use a combination of crimini and portobello mushrooms, and go with wild rice or brown rice as a grain. They taste souper!

1 tablespoon olive oil

1 medium yellow or white onion, chopped

1 tablespoon Trader Joe's Reduced Sodium Soy Sauce

4 to 5 cups chopped mushrooms

2 tablespoons unbleached all-purpose flour

3 cups water, divided

1 cup cooked grain

VEGAN

In a medium stockpot, heat the oil over medium heat. Add the onion and cook until it begins to soften and becomes fragrant, about 3 minutes. Add the soy sauce and mushrooms and cook until the mushrooms begin to soften and release juices, about 5 minutes, stirring often. Add the flour and ½ cup of the water and whisk until the mixture begins to thicken, about 2 minutes. Incorporate the remaining 2½ cups water and cook until heated through and the mushrooms are tender, about 10 minutes. Using an immersion blender or a countertop blender, process ½ cup of the soup until creamy. Return to pot and mix to combine. Add the grain and cook until heated through, about 3 minutes.

MAKES: 4 to 5 servings

AFRICAN PEANUT STEW

Sweet, spicy, and peanutty...this stew has it all. Inspired by the traditional African flavors of sweet potatoes and peanuts (a worthy combo, indeed), this stew is creamy and delicious, with a little kick from the cayenne and a crunch from some peanuts tossed on top.

2 tablespoons olive oil

1 small white or yellow onion, diced

2 cloves garlic, minced

3 cups sweet potatoes, peeled and cut into a 1-inch dice (from about 2 large sweet potatoes)

1 (15-ounce) can Trader Joe's White Kidney Beans, drained and rinsed

1 (14.5-ounce) can Trader Joe's Organic Tomatoes Diced & No Salt Added

½ cup Trader Joe's Light Coconut Milk (canned)

⅓ cup Trader Joe's Creamy Valencia Peanut Butter

½ cup water

¼ teaspoon salt

¼ to 1 teaspoon ground cayenne pepper (depending on preferred spice level)

2 cups Very Versatile Quinoa (page 118)

¼ cup chopped fresh cilantro, for garnish

¼ cup roasted unsalted peanuts, for garnish

VEGAN, GLUTEN-FREE

In a large stockpot, heat the olive oil on medium low heat. Add the onion and cook until translucent, about 5 minutes. Add the garlic and cook until fragrant, about 2 minutes longer. Add the sweet potatoes, white kidney beans, tomatoes with their juices, coconut milk, peanut butter, and water, and increase the heat to medium. Bring to a simmer and cook until the coconut milk, peanut butter, and water come together as a sauce, then add the salt and cayenne. Reduce heat to medium low and cook, covered and stirring often, until the sweet potatoes are tender, 20 to 25 minutes. If the sauce reduces, add a little more water. Once the potatoes are tender, remove from the heat. Serve the stew over ½-cup portions of the quinoa and garnish with the cilantro and peanuts.

MAKES: 4 servings

VARIATION: Make it an African peanut soup by chopping the sweet potatoes to a smaller ½-inch dice and increasing the liquids to ¾ cup coconut milk, ½ cup peanut butter, and 1 cup water. Mix the whole peanuts in with the soup and mix in 1 cup of quinoa at the very end. Yum!

THREE-BEAN CHILI

Packed with vegetables and fiber, this chili is the first hearty meal to emerge from my kitchen as soon as the temperature drops. Like most things with layers of flavors, chili is actually even better the second day.

2 tablespoons olive oil

1 medium yellow onion, diced

2 cloves garlic, minced

¼ cup chili powder

1 tablespoon Trader Joe's Unsweetened Cocoa Powder

2 teaspoons smoked paprika

2 teaspoons ground cumin

1 teaspoon garlic powder

1 teaspoon sea salt

1 (12-ounce) bag Trader Joe's Cut Butternut Squash

1 (14.5-ounce) can Trader Joe's Organic Tomatoes Diced & Fire Roasted with Organic Green Chiles

1 (15-ounce) can Trader Joe's Organic Black Beans, drained and rinsed

1 (15-ounce) can Trader Joe's Organic Pinto Beans, drained and rinsed

1 (15-ounce) can Trader Joe's Organic Kidney Beans, drained and rinsed

3 tablespoons tomato paste

½ cup water

1 cup frozen Trader Joe's Organic Super Sweet Cut Corn

guacamole, shredded cheese, and sour cream, to serve (optional)

VEGAN, GLUTEN-FREE

In a large stockpot, heat the olive oil and sauté the onion until translucent, about 5 minutes. Add the garlic and mix until fragrant. Add the chili powder, cocoa, paprika, cumin, garlic powder, and salt, and mix to combine. Add the butternut squash, canned tomatoes, all of the beans, tomato paste, and water. Mix to combine.

Bring the soup to a simmer and cover with a lid. Stirring occasionally, simmer until the butternut squash is tender, about 25 minutes. Add the sweet corn and adjust the flavor to taste, adding water if needed. Cook until heated through, about 5 more minutes. Serve with toppings of choice.

MAKES: 4 large servings

CREAMY GNOCCHI DUMPLING SOUP

This soup is creamy without being heavy, comforting without requiring a nap. Gnocchi are the easiest way to get tender dumplings with the least amount of effort.

2 tablespoons olive oil

2 large leeks, white and light-green parts only, rinsed and thinly sliced

1 small yellow onion, chopped

3 tablespoons all-purpose flour

2 cups milk

2 cups water

1 (12-ounce) bag Trader Joe's Cauliflower Florets, roughly chopped

1 bay leaf

1 teaspoon sea salt

½ teaspoon pepper

1½ cups shredded sharp white cheddar cheese

1 (16-ounce) container Trader Joe's Gnocchi

1 tablespoon fresh lemon juice

chopped fresh chives, to serve

VEGAN, GLUTEN-FREE

Heat the olive oil in a stockpot over medium heat. Add the leeks and onion and cook until translucent, about 5 minutes. Sprinkle the flour over the leeks and onion to coat and cook, stirring often, until the flour is toasted and golden, about 2 minutes. Slowly whisk in the milk and water and then add the cauliflower, bay leaf, salt, and pepper. Remove the bay leaf and transfer the soup to a blender, pureeing until it is smooth. Return the pureed soup to the pot and add the cheese, mixing until it is melted. Adjust and season to taste.

Add the gnocchi and reduce the heat to low, cooking until tender, about 5 minutes. Add a drizzle of lemon juice and incorporate. Adjust the seasoning to taste. Serve with a sprinkle of chopped chives on top.

MAKES: 4 large servings

Sandwiches

Nothing satisfies quite like a sammich and soup. Or a sammich and a salad. Or just a warm, toasty, gooey sammich all on its own. Except that, if one is to be proper, they must be called sandwiches. Tasty, tasty sandwiches.

ALL ABOUT AVOCADO SANDWICHES

This sandwich has some Mexican flair, but holds a tantalizing taste that's all its own. It's easy to make and multiply, so be sure to share with friends!

4 slices sandwich bread of choice

2 tablespoons unsalted butter

6 tablespoons Trader Joe's Avocado's Number Guacamole

½ (12-ounce) jar Trader Joe's Fire-Roasted Red Peppers, blotted dry

⅓ cup crumbled feta cheese

¼ cup fresh cilantro

Lightly butter 1 side each of the 4 slices of bread. On the unbuttered side of 2 of the slices, divide the guacamole, spreading 3 tablespoons on each of the slices. Layer the peppers, feta, and cilantro and top with the unbuttered side of the other slices of bread. Heat a medium sauté pan or skillet over medium heat and grill the sandwiches until golden brown, about 4 minutes on each side.

MAKES: 2 sandwiches

VEGAN OPTION: Replace the butter with Trader Joe's Vegan Buttery Spread. Omit the feta or replace with Tangy Vegan Cheese Spread (page 49).

HAWAIIAN BBQ SANDWICHES

Fontina, Swiss, or mild cheddar make some of the best cheese additions.

2 tablespoons olive oil

½ small yellow or white onion, diced

1 (14½-ounce) can Trader Joe's Organic Garbanzo Beans, drained and rinsed

⅓ cup Trader Joe's Bold & Smoky Kansas City Style Barbecue Sauce

½ cup Trader Joe's Frozen Pineapple Tidbits, thawed

4 buns or rolls, split

4 slices mild cheese

In a small saucepan over medium low heat, heat the oil. Add the onion and sauté until translucent, about 5 minutes. Add the garbanzos and barbecue sauce. Cook until the sauce begins to coat the garbanzos, about 5 minutes. Remove from the heat and add the pineapple tidbits. Spread the garbanzo mixture evenly on the bottom of each split roll. Top with the cheese. Place under a broiler until the cheese is melted, 1 to 3 minutes. Place the top of each roll on top of the melted cheese.

MAKES: 4 sandwiches

VEGAN OPTION: Omit the cheese or use a vegan cheese substitute.

BEET-OF-YOUR-OWN DRUMMUS SANDWICHES

This is a surefire win for beet lovers. And with TJ's prepackaged, prepared beets, it's easy to make. For the hummus, opt for any of TJ's varieties; roasted red pepper is my personal favorite for this recipe.

1 (8-ounce) package Trader Joe's Steamed and Peeled Baby Beets

1 cup hummus

4 buns or rolls, or 8 slices bread

lettuce, as needed

⅓ cup crumbled goat cheese or blue cheese

Drain the package of beets and slice into ¼-inch-thick slices. Spread an even layer of hummus on 1 side of each slice of the bread. Add a layer of lettuce over 2 of the slices, and top with a nice layer of beet slices. Top with a sprinkle of cheese and the remaining 2 slices of bread.

MAKES: 4 sandwiches

VEGAN OPTION: Omit the cheese or substitute a spread of Tangy Vegan Cheese Spread (page 49) on 1 side of the sandwich.

ULTIMATE TOFU SANDWICHES

These sandwiches see a lot of play in my house. The baked tofu is flavorful on its own— but when paired with tangy mustard, creamy hummus, and some helpful vegetables, these sandwiches become amazing. They make great road trip or beach fare.

4 slices whole wheat bread

2 to 3 tablespoons Trader Joe's Deli Style Spicy Brown Mustard

⅓ cup Trader Joe's Garlic Hummus Dip

handful of mixed greens

4 slices Baked Tofu (page 143)

½ cup sliced tomatoes, divided

4 slices Trader Joe's Organic Kosher Sandwich Pickles, divided

VEGAN

On 1 side of 2 bread slices, spread the mustard. Spread the hummus on 1 side of the other 2 slices. Place a solid layer of mixed greens on top of the hummus side of each sandwich. Top the mixed greens with 2 slices of tofu each. Top the tofu with tomato slices and 2 pickle slices each. Top each sandwich with the mustard side of the bread.

MAKES: 2 sandwiches

PACKED PITA SANDWICHES

A pita offers a good way to wrangle sandwich fixings that might otherwise go rogue: shredded carrots, olives, a dressing. Trader Joe's pita varieties vary by region, but it's very likely that you will have several options to pick from. Use big pitas, as listed in the recipe, or try Trader Joe's Mini Pitas for kid-friendly bites and mini sandwiches. Just be sure to get the ones that have pockets you can fill, not the flatbread variety. You can substitute TJ's black olive tapenade in this recipe too, which brings out a great flavor.

2 Trader Joe's Pita Bread

2 tablespoons Trader Joe's Olive Tapenade with Kalamata & Chalikidiki Olives

½ cup salad greens

⅓ cup shredded carrots

½ cup Trader Joe's Organic Garbanzo Beans, drained and rinsed

½ cup Trader Joe's Shredded Mozzarella Cheese or shredded provolone cheese

4 tablespoons Trader Joe's Green Goddess Salad Dressing

avocado slices, to serve (optional)

Cut the tops cut off each pita just enough to make a 2½-to 3-inch opening. Heat up the pitas in a microwave or a 300°F oven just until soft, about 15 seconds in the microwave or 1 to 2 minutes in the oven. This will make them more pliable and easier to fill. Using a butter knife, carefully open up each pita, making it a pocket. Spread 1 tablespoon of the tapenade on 1 side of each pita pocket. Divide and stuff in the greens, carrots, and beans. Sprinkle the cheese on top of the beans and then drizzle 2 tablespoons of the dressing into each pita. Top with the avocado, if using.

MAKES: 2 sandwiches, doubles easily

VEGAN OPTION: Omit the cheese or replace with Tangy Vegan Cheese Spread (page 49), applied on the side opposite of the tapenade.

MCNOMMY BREAKFAST SANDWICHES

The breakfast sandwich is an American staple, but the typical offerings at drive-throughs and gas stations can be pretty gross. Greasy and processed, they aren't exactly the best a.m. fuel. These tasty sandwiches are so delicious, you will be excited to get out of bed in the morning.

4 Savory Muffins (page 20)

2 tablespoons olive oil, divided

4 eggs

⅓ cup Trader Joe's Shredded 3 Cheese Blend, divided

4 Trader Joe's Vegetable Sausage Patties (in the frozen section), thawed

Split each muffin in half, like a bun. Heat the olive oil in a small sauté pan or skillet over medium low heat. Whisk each egg in a small bowl 1 at a time. Add 1 egg at a time to the pan and cook, scrambled, until cooked through, then sprinkle the top with cheese. Essentially, you are making a small, basic omelet. Fold in half and place an egg on top of each split muffin. In the same pan, heat the remaining olive oil and warm each vegetable patty, cooking on each side for about 2 minutes. Place the patties on top of the eggs and top with the other half of each muffin.

MAKES: 4 sandwiches

VEGAN OPTION: Replace the eggs with Trader Joe's Simply Eggless (per the label) and use one of TJ's many refrigerated or frozen veggie sausage options.

GRILLED CHOCOLATE, PB, AND 'NANA BLISS

Sweet bananas, melty chocolate chips, and slightly salty peanut butter come together in perfect harmony.

2 to 3 tablespoons unsalted butter

4 slices whole grain bread

⅓ cup Trader Joe's Valencia Peanut Butter, divided

¼ cup semisweet chocolate chips, divided

1 ripe banana, sliced into long slices, divided

Heat a medium sauté pan or skillet over medium heat. Butter 1 side of each piece of bread. On 1 unbuttered side of 1 piece of bread, spread the peanut butter. Sprinkle with half of the chocolate chips, then top with half of the banana slices. Place the other piece of bread on top, buttered-side out. Grill on each side until browned, 2 to 3 minutes. Repeat with the remaining ingredients.

MAKES: 2 sandwiches

VEGAN OPTION: Use Trader Joe's Vegan Buttery Spread in place of the butter.

TEMPEH WRAP

I love tempeh crumbles. I eat them on their own, of course, but I also like them mixed up in my Sweet Potato Colcannon (page 122) and I LOVE them in this wrap. Versatility rules.

2 Trader Joe's Whole Wheat Flour Tortillas

¼ cup cream cheese or Trader Joe's Reduced Fat Mayonnaise

¼ cup Trader Joe's Pitted Kalamata Olives, chopped

1 cup Trader Joe's Organics Baby Romaine

⅓ cup shredded carrots

1 cup warm Tempeh Crumbles (page 134)

Warm the tortillas in a dry pan over low heat or in the microwave on high power for about 15 seconds. Spread the base with a healthy schmear of cream cheese or mayonnaisennaise. Sprinkle on the chopped olives, 2 to 3 olives worth per tortilla. Layer with the lettuce and shredded vegetables, and top with warm tempeh crumbles. Wrap and serve.

MAKES: 2 wraps

VEGAN OPTION: Use Trader Joe's Reduced Fat Mayonnaise, which is vegan, or Trader Joe's nondairy spread.

FIGGY BLUE SANDWICHES

This sandwich was inspired by a similar 'wich from an upscale cheese shop in St. Paul, Minnesota. Thankfully, TJ's makes it affordable to eat fancy sandwiches in the comfort of your home, while you're dressed in sweats, free from the risk of being judged by any cheese shop owners. The fig butter called for in this recipe is ridiculously rich and pairs perfectly with the tangy blue cheese.

2 large slices fresh, crusty bread

⅓ cup Trader Joe's Fig Butter, divided

handful Trader Joe's Organics Baby Romaine or other greens, divided

4 to 6 thin slices blue cheese, divided

Slice the crusty bread in half. Liberally spread the fig butter on both sides of the inside of the bread. Layer the romaine or other greens and then the blue cheese on each sandwich.

MAKES: 2 sandwiches

VEGAN OPTION: Substitute the blue cheese with Tangy Vegan Cheese Spread (page 49).

GROWN-UP GRILLED CHEESE

This grilled cheese is a delicious twist on tradition. My recommendation is to get the sharpest cheese you can in order to really bring out the contrast with the jam and apple slices. Galas are my favorite apples to use in these sandwiches.

2 to 3 tablespoons unsalted butter

4 slices sourdough bread

4 slices extra-sharp cheddar cheese, divided

⅓ cup Trader Joe's Organic Reduced Sugar Apricot Preserves, divided

1 large, sweet apple, cut into thin slices

Heat a medium sauté pan or skillet over medium heat. Butter 1 side of each piece of bread. Spread the jam on 2 unbuttered sides and top with half of the apple slices. Lay the cheese on the other unbuttered sides. Fold each sandwich together and grill until browned and the cheese is melted, 2 to 3 minutes on each side.

MAKES: 2 sandwiches

VEGAN OPTION: Use Trader Joe's Vegan Buttery Spread in place of the butter and substitute a vegan cheese.

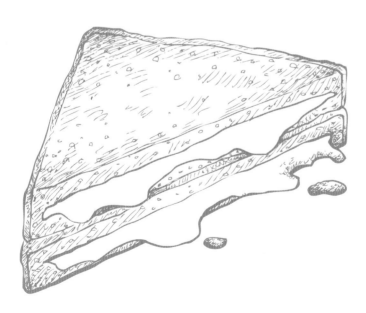

BIRBIGS ENGLISH MUFFIN PIZZA

One of my all-time favorite comedians is Mike Birbiglia, who likes to boast of his mad English-muffin-pizza-making skills when referencing reasons why girls should like him. I decided to honor him in style with this English muffin pizza recipe, perfect for sharing with the good-looking mate it will surely attract. Sprinkle on dried basil instead of fresh for a delicious variation.

1 Trader Joe's Disraeli & Gladstone British Style Multigrain English Muffin

2 tablespoons Trader Joe's Fat Free Pizza Sauce

1 medium Roma tomato, sliced

2 slices mozzarella cheese

4 fresh basil leaves (optional)

Slice the English muffin in half. Spread 1 tablespoon of the pizza sauce on each side. Top each with a slice of tomato and a slice of cheese. Toast in a toaster oven, on a pan, until the cheese is melted and any exposed muffin is browned, 3 to 5 minutes. Alternatively, in a regular oven, with a rack set about 6 inches from the heat source, broil for about 3 minutes, checking frequently. Remove the mini pizzas from the oven and top with fresh basil, if using. Eat all while reveling in your mad English-muffin-pizza-making skills.

MAKES: 1 sandwich

VEGAN OPTION: Omit the mozzarella and replace with vegan cheese.

ROASTED VEGETABLE IN-A-FLASH SANDWICHES

If you love roasted eggplant, you'll love the Roasted Eggplant Spread recipe on page 48. And more than that, you'll love what you can do with the leftovers—make this amazing sandwich.

2 to 3 tablespoons unsalted butter

4 slices sourdough bread

¼ cup Roasted Eggplant Spread (page 48)

6 to 8 slices Trader Giotto's Misto alla Griglia (in the frozen section), thawed

2 to 3 thin slices fresh mozzarella

Heat a medium sauté pan or skillet over medium heat. Butter 1 side of 2 pieces of bread. Spread the eggplant on 1 of the unbuttered sides, then add half of the slices of vegetables from the Misto alla Griglia. Top with the mozzarella and the other slice of bread, buttered-side facing out. Grill until browned and the cheese is melted, 2 to 3 minutes on each side. Repeat with the other sandwich.

MAKES: 2 sandwiches

· ·

VEGAN OPTION: Use Trader Joe's Vegan Buttery Spread in place of the butter and substitute a vegan cheese.

· ·

PULLED JACKFRUIT SANDWICHES

Who needs pulled pork when you can have pulled jackfruit?

2 tablespoons olive oil

1 small yellow onion, chopped

½ teaspoon sea salt

1 (20-ounce) can Trader Joe's Green Jackfruit in Brine, drained, rinsed, and roughly chopped

½ cup water

½ cup Trader Joe's Organic Ketchup

⅓ cup apple cider vinegar

2 tablespoons brown sugar

2 cloves garlic, crushed

1 teaspoon Dijon mustard

½ teaspoon smoked paprika

½ teaspoon ground cumin

Trader Joe's sandwich buns of your choice

Trader Joe's Organic Coleslaw Kit (optional)

salt and pepper, to taste

VEGAN, GLUTEN-FREE

In a large skillet, heat the olive oil over medium heat. Add the onion and salt and sauté, stirring often, until the onion is slightly translucent, about 3 minutes. Add the jackfruit and the water, and bring to a simmer. Cover and let simmer for about 10 minutes, until the jackfruit begins to get tender.

Add the ketchup, apple cider vinegar, brown sugar, garlic, Dijon mustard, paprika, and cumin, and mix to combine. Bring to a boil and then cover and reduce to a simmer. Cook for about 20 minutes, until the sauce is thick and the jackfruit is tender. Break apart using a potato masher. Season with salt and pepper to taste. Serve on toasted buns. Add pickles or some chopped vegetables from the Trader Joe's Organic Coleslaw Kit on top of the jackfruit for a nice crunch.

MAKES: 4 to 6 sandwiches

Sides

Sides can often get neglected. Without a little planning, your lovely main course might be accompanied by frozen vegetables or a side of chips! Thankfully, this chapter is full of delicious side dishes that shine all on their own.

- TAHINI BROCCOLINI
- TAHINI SAUCE
- SHALLOTS AND SPINACH
- SWEET BRUSSELS SPROUTS SAUTÉ
- ROASTED BRUSSELS SPROUTS
- DIJON VEGETABLE TOSS
- ALMOND-GLAZED GREEN BEANS
- ROASTED GREEN ONIONS
- BERRY BALSAMIC GLAZE
- CAULIFLOWER GRATIN
- AMAZING TUSCAN BAKED POTATOES
- PESTO'D POTATOES
- VERY VERSATILE QUINOA
- BESTO PESTO
- SESAME KALE
- MINTED PEAS AND CARROTS
- SWEET POTATO COLCANNON
- ROASTED FENNEL
- COCONUT CURRY POLENTA

TAHINI BROCCOLINI

Broccolini becomes smoky and sweet when roasted or grilled. The heads of each spear soak up the tangy tahini sauce, making this dish seem almost indecent, it's so indulgent.

2 (8-ounce) packages Trader Joe's Broccolini, ends slightly trimmed

1 tablespoon olive oil

salt and pepper

1 recipe Tahini Sauce (recipe below)

VEGAN, GLUTEN-FREE

Preheat an outdoor or countertop grill to a medium heat, about 350°F. You can also use a panini press, which is what I use for this recipe. Brush the broccolini with the olive oil and sprinkle with salt and pepper. Grill until the stalks are tender but still crisp, 8 to 10 minutes. Remove from the heat and serve with the tahini sauce. If you don't have a grill or panini press, you can roast the broccolini in the oven on a baking sheet lined with parchment paper or foil. Preheat the oven to 425°F and roast until tender, 10 to 12 minutes.

MAKES: 3 to 4 servings

TAHINI SAUCE

This tahini sauce is classic and versatile—a wonderful addition to anyone's repertoire.

½ cup Trader Joe's Tahini Sauce

⅓ cup water, plus more if needed

¼ cup fresh lemon juice

1 teaspoon lemon zest

1 tablespoon olive oil

1 small garlic clove, crushed

½ teaspoon sea salt

VEGAN, GLUTEN-FREE

Whisk together the tahini, water, lemon juice, lemon zest, olive oil, garlic, and salt in a small bowl. Whisk until it's emulsified, and adjust the salt and lemon juice to taste. Thin out with extra water if needed.

MAKES: 1 cup

SHALLOTS AND SPINACH

Shallots are delicious! Not only are they available at Trader Joe's, they're a steal, which makes it easy to incorporate this tasty vegetable into your diet even if you're on a tight budget. In this simple side dish, fresh spinach is a lovely backdrop for the shallots' natural flavor.

2 tablespoons unsalted butter

4 shallots, peeled and sliced into thin rounds

1 (6-ounce) bag Trader Joe's Organics Baby Spinach

salt and pepper

GLUTEN-FREE

In a medium sauté pan or skillet with a lid, melt the butter over medium low heat. Add the shallots and cook, stirring often, until golden and soft, about 5 minutes. Add the spinach and mix, then cover with a lid. Let the spinach steam until just wilted, but still vibrantly green, 2 to 3 minutes, stirring occasionally. Remove from the heat and season to taste with salt and pepper.

MAKES: 3 to 4 servings

VEGAN OPTION: Replace the butter with Trader Joe's Vegan Buttery Spread.

SWEET BRUSSELS SPROUTS SAUTÉ

This sauté perks up brussels sprouts with an unconventional touch of sweetness and crunch. Eat it warm or cold; either way it's delicious. For the holidays, dust with cinnamon and serve as a Thanksgiving side.

3 tablespoons olive oil

⅓ cup dried cranberries

1 (10-ounce) bag Trader Joe's Shaved Brussels Sprouts

1 medium Gala or Fuji apple, peeled and shredded

2 tablespoons lemon juice

¼ cup Trader Joe's Raw Slivered Almonds or Trader Joe's Unsalted Dry Toasted Pecan Pieces

VEGAN, GLUTEN-FREE

In a large sauté pan or skillet with a lid, heat the oil over medium low heat. Add the cranberries and cook for about 1 minute, to plump. Add the shaved brussels sprouts and toss to coat with the olive oil. Cover and reduce the heat to low. Toss the brussels sprouts mixture every minute or 2, just until vibrantly green and slightly tender; you don't want it to wilt. Remove from the heat and mix in the apple and lemon. Top with the nuts before serving.

MAKES: 4 to 6 servings

COOK'S NOTE: If TJ's is out of the Shaved Brussels Sprouts, you can use their 16-ounce bag of whole brussels sprouts. Cut off and diskard the bottoms and then finely chop.

ROASTED BRUSSELS SPROUTS

Forget your misconceptions of mushy, boiled brussels sprouts and prepare to be wowed. Roasting brussels sprouts showcases their naturally delicious flavor. The added bonus: they're so simple to prepare, they almost make themselves.

2 tablespoons olive oil

2 cloves garlic, minced

1 teaspoon balsamic vinegar

1 (16-ounce) bag Trader Joe's Brussels Sprouts, ends trimmed and large ones halved

salt and pepper

VEGAN, GLUTEN-FREE

Preheat the oven to 400°F and line a baking sheet with parchment paper. In a large bowl, combine the oil, garlic, and vinegar. Add the brussels sprouts and toss to coat. Spread in a single layer on the prepared baking sheet. Bake until the brussels sprouts feel tender when pierced with a fork, 20 to 25 minutes, stirring halfway through the cooking time. Season to taste with salt and pepper.

MAKES: 4 servings

DIJON VEGETABLE TOSS

This vegetable combination has it all—creamy potatoes, crunchy green beans, soft and crisp baby lettuce, and a tangy Dijon mustard sauce. Bring this to your next potluck and class up the joint a bit!

1 (16-ounce) bag Trader Joe's Teeny Tiny Potatoes

8 ounces fresh Trader Joe's Green Beans, ends trimmed

4 cups Trader Joe's Organics Baby Spinach

2½ teaspoons Dijon mustard

3 tablespoons white balsamic vinegar

2 tablespoons olive oil

2 cloves garlic, minced

salt and pepper

VEGAN, GLUTEN-FREE

Place the potatoes in a large pot filled with water and bring to a boil over high heat. Reduce the temperature to medium and let simmer until the potatoes are tender when pierced with a fork, 10 to 15 minutes, depending on the size of the potatoes. Once tender, add the green beans to the pot and cook until the beans are still crisp but are vibrantly green, about 2 minutes. While the potatoes are cooking, place the spinach in a large bowl. In a small bowl, whisk together the Dijon mustard, vinegar, oil, and garlic. When the potatoes and beans are done, drain well and add to the bowl with the spinach. Toss the dressing with the vegetables. Some of the spinach will wilt a little and some will stay crisp; this will add a nice variance of texture to the dish. Season to taste with salt and pepper, and serve warm or cold.

MAKES: 4 to 6 servings

COOK'S NOTE: If you don't have white balsamic vinegar, regular balsamic will work just as well; just reduce the amount by 1 teaspoon. White balsamic has a slightly milder flavor.

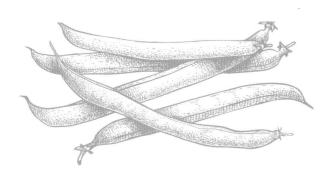

ALMOND-GLAZED GREEN BEANS

Trader Joe's has a great selection of green beans, some of which are already trimmed, which will make your prep time all the easier. These green beans are a little salty, a little sticky, and a little crunchy—which makes them entirely delicious.

1 tablespoon unsalted butter

1 tablespoon Trader Joe's Reduced Sodium Soy Sauce

1 teaspoon Trader Joe's Organic Evaporated Cane Juice Sugar

4 cups green beans, ends trimmed

¼ cup sliced or slivered almonds

salt and pepper

In a large sauté pan, heat the butter over medium low heat. Add the soy sauce and the sugar and whisk well, dissolving the sugar. Add the green beans, toss to coat, and cover, reducing the heat to low. Continue to occasionally stir the beans to keep them coated in the mixture, and cook until tender when pierced with a fork but still crisp, 5 to 7 minutes, depending on the thickness of the beans. Serve the beans with the almonds sprinkled on top.

MAKES: 4 servings

VEGAN OPTION: Use Trader Joe's Vegan Buttery Spread in place of the butter.

ROASTED GREEN ONIONS

These onions are a perfect solution for what to do with the leftovers when you buy a bag of green onions and only use two stalks. Make these tasty onions and top with Berry Balsamic Glaze (recipe follows). Yum!

8 to 10 green onion stalks, trimmed

2 tablespoons olive oil

salt and pepper

1 lemon, cut into wedges

Berry Balsamic Glaze (recipe follows)

VEGAN, GLUTEN-FREE

Preheat the oven to 375°F and line a baking sheet with parchment paper. Brush both sides of the onions with olive oil and place on the prepared sheet. Sprinkle with salt and pepper. Roast until tender, 8 to 10 minutes. Remove from the oven and squeeze a bit of fresh lemon juice onto the onions. Serve with the berry balsamic glaze drizzled on top.

MAKES: 3 to 4 servings

BERRY BALSAMIC GLAZE

This glaze is thick, sweet, and tangy. It's delicious drizzled over salad or roasted vegetables. If you're feeling a little saucy, try it over vanilla ice cream. Delicious.

¼ cup thawed Trader Joe's Very Cherry Berry Blend (in the frozen section)

1 cup balsamic vinegar

VEGAN, GLUTEN-FREE

In a food processor, puree the berry blend. In a small saucepan, whisk together the vinegar and the berry puree. Simmer over medium heat until reduced by half, about 15 minutes. Remove from the heat and let cool; it will continue to thicken and will easily coat the back of a spoon.

MAKES: ½ cup of glaze

CAULIFLOWER GRATIN

Cauliflower takes the place of starchy potatoes in this gratin, giving you a lighter and quicker-cooking side that will satisfy your creamy-cheesy cravings. When they're in stock, substitute TJ's Gourmet Fried Onion Pieces for the bread crumbs.

1 (12-ounce) bag Trader Joe's Cauliflower Florets

1 tablespoon olive oil

2 cloves garlic, minced

2 teaspoons fresh thyme

1½ cups Trader Joe's Shredded 3 Cheese Blend

1½ cups milk

salt and pepper

1 cup Trader Joe's Japanese Style Panko Breadcrumbs

Preheat the oven to 375°F and lightly grease an 8 x 8-inch casserole dish. Slice the cauliflower into ¼-inch-thick slices. There will be crumbly bits; that's fine because you can still incorporate them. Heat the olive oil in a small saucepan on medium low heat. Add the garlic and cook until fragrant, about 1 minute. Add the thyme and mix. Add the cheese and whisk in the milk, mixing until the cheese has melted into the mixture. Season to taste with salt and pepper. Remove from the heat. Set 1 layer of the cauliflower slices in the bottom of the casserole dish. Pour half of the milk-cheese mixture over top. Add the remaining cauliflower slices and any crumbly bits and top with the remaining cheese sauce. Top the casserole with the bread crumbs. Bake until bubbly and the crumbs are browned, and the cauliflower is tender when pierced with a fork, 25 to 30 minutes.

MAKES: 8 to 10 servings

VEGAN OPTION: Replace the cheese and milk with nondairy equivalents.

AMAZING TUSCAN BAKED POTATOES

These potatoes are incredibly easy and super addictive; I recommend making a couple of extras. Trust me—you'll need them.

4 large baking potatoes, scrubbed

½ cup Trader Joe's Tuscan Italian Dressing

½ cup Trader Giotto's Bruschetta

VEGAN

Preheat the oven to 375°F. Slice each potato into ½-inch slices, but keep them assembled in their respective potato shapes. Place each potato on a generous piece of aluminum foil. Drizzle 2 tablespoons of the dressing over each potato, getting it between the slices as well. Wrap them up in the foil, with the foil seams on the top, and bake until the potato slices are tender when pierced with a fork, 45 to 60 minutes. Let the potatoes cool slightly before serving with the bruschetta on top.

MAKES: 4 servings

PESTO'D POTATOES

Holy geez. These potatoes will blow your mind. They're crisp on the edges, creamy in the center, and coated in a thick and fragrant glaze of fresh pesto. These potatoes are a great addition to a brunch menu.

1½ (1-pound) bags Trader Joe's Teeny Tiny Potatoes or other small, fingerling-style potatoes

3 tablespoons olive oil

2 cloves garlic, cut into thin slices

2 teaspoons lemon juice

salt and pepper

1½ cups Besto Pesto (page 119)

VEGAN, GLUTEN-FREE

Cut any larger potatoes in half to ensure a consistent cooking time. In a large sauté pan or skillet, heat the oil over medium low heat. Add the garlic and cook for 1 minute before adding the potatoes. Add just enough water to cover the bottom of the pan, cover with a lid, and increase the heat to medium. Cook the potatoes, stirring often, until tender when pierced with a fork, 10 to 15 minutes. As needed, add a splash of water to deglaze the bottom of the pan and release any brown bits. Remove the pan with the potatoes from the heat and add the lemon juice and a bit of salt and pepper. Add the pesto and stir to combine, covering the potatoes with a thick coating. Serve warm.

MAKES: 4 to 5 servings

VERY VERSATILE QUINOA

If you don't already eat quinoa, prepare to have a new addiction. While it's used as a grain, it's actually a seed. High in protein and fiber, quinoa is delicious and fits gracefully into a variety of meals. It grows coated in its own natural insect repellent, so be sure to rinse it well before cooking. Cook it up basic style, like instructed below, or try one of my variations. It will quickly become a staple in your diet! Note the specific amount of water or broth given; this is my trick to getting quinoa to be perfectly fluffy.

1 cup Trader Joe's Organic White Quinoa

2 cups less 1 tablespoon water or Trader Joe's Organic Hearty Vegetable Broth

VEGAN, GLUTEN-FREE

Rinse the quinoa well. Bring the water or broth to a simmer in a medium pot over medium high heat. Add the quinoa and reduce the heat to medium low. Cook covered, without stirring, until the water is absorbed, 10 to 15 minutes, depending on depth of your pot. Remove from the heat and let the quinoa cool for at least 10 minutes before fluffing with a fork.

MAKES: 2 cups

ORANGE CREAM QUINOA VARIATION: For a sweet quinoa treat, replace ¼ of the liquid with Trader Joe's Light Coconut Milk (canned) and use water for the remainder. Add the zest of 1 small orange. Serve for breakfast with some nuts and dried fruit.

INDIAN QUINOA VARIATION: Whisk 1 teaspoon of curry powder into the water just before adding the quinoa. Optionally, you can also substitute ¼ of the liquid with Trader Joe's Light Coconut Milk (canned).

QUINOA PUDDING VARIATION: For a spin on rice pudding, make the basic recipe, but with milk instead of water (be careful not to boil). At the end, add 1 teaspoon of ground cinnamon and ¼ cup of raisins. Add a dab of butter or Trader Joe's Vegan Buttery Spread to the individual servings and an additional splash of milk, if desired.

BESTO PESTO

This pesto comes together quickly and is so delicious. It's fantastic as a coating for potatoes (Pesto'd Potatoes, page 117), as a filling in a calzone (Quick Calzones, page 135), or even as a dip with an appetizer (Fantastic Fry Bread, page 42).

1 (2.5-ounce) container Trader Joe's Fresh Basil

2 small cloves garlic

¼ cup Trader Joe's Raw California Walnut Pieces

1 teaspoon lemon juice

3 to 4 tablespoons olive oil

VEGAN, GLUTEN-FREE

In the bowl of a food processor or blender, combine the basil, garlic, and walnuts, and pulse to a thick puree. Add the lemon juice and olive oil 1 teaspoon at a time, stopping occasionally to check the consistency, until it becomes a creamy paste.

MAKES: 1 to 1½ cups

SESAME KALE

This kale is simple but still exotic enough to perk up any meal.

1 to 2 tablespoons olive oil

2 cloves garlic, minced

½ to 1 teaspoon Trader Joe's Toasted Sesame Oil

4 cups Trader Joe's Kale

1 tablespoon water

1 tablespoon sesame seeds

VEGAN, GLUTEN-FREE

In a medium sauté pan, heat the olive oil over medium heat. Add the garlic and cook until fragrant, about 2 minutes. Add the sesame oil and then the kale and toss to coat. Add the water and cover with a lid, reducing the heat to low, until the kale is vibrant and tender, 5 to 10 minutes. Remove from the heat and sprinkle with sesame seeds.

MAKES: 2 servings

MINTED PEAS AND CARROTS

This new spin on the classic peas and carrots side dish takes it up a notch, making it respectable for adults to indulge. Kids will love it too!

2 cups sliced carrots, cut into ¼-inch-thick coins

2 cups fresh peas or Trader Joe's Fresh Harvest Petite Peas (in the frozen section)

2 tablespoons unsalted butter

1 tablespoon chopped fresh mint

salt and pepper

GLUTEN-FREE

Fill a large pot with water and bring to a boil over medium high heat. Add the carrots and cook until tender, about 3 minutes. Add the peas and cook for 2 minutes longer if frozen, only 1 minute if fresh. Drain and return the vegetables to the pot, removed from any heat. Add the butter and mint, and mix to combine and coat the vegetables with the butter. Season to taste with salt and pepper.

MAKES: 4 servings

VEGAN OPTION: Replace the butter with Trader Joe's Vegan Buttery Spread.

SWEET POTATO COLCANNON

Colcannon is an Irish dish traditionally made with mashed potatoes and kale, but this version uses sweet potatoes, one of my favorite root vegetables. With the earthy kale, which TJ's conveniently has chopped and bagged for you, this dish provides super-healthy comfort food with minimal effort.

1½ pounds sweet potatoes, peeled, and chopped

2 cups Trader Joe's Kale

2 to 3 tablespoons unsalted butter

2 to 4 tablespoons milk

GLUTEN-FREE

Place the sweet potatoes in a large saucepan and cover with a couple of inches of water. Bring to a boil over high heat and cook until the potatoes are tender when pierced with a fork, 15 to 20 minutes. Add the kale and cover. Cook for only 1 minute before draining and removing from the heat. Add the butter and milk and mash together, adding more milk as needed, until the mixture is smooth and the kale is incorporated. Serve with an additional dollop of butter on top of each serving.

MAKES: 4 servings

....

VEGAN OPTION: Replace the butter and milk with their nondairy equivalents.

....

ROASTED FENNEL

This recipe centers on the hearty and flavorful herb, fennel. It will serve as an unexpected complement to whatever you pair it with. I suggest serving it alongside a pasta dish, such as Olive My Love Pasta (page 131).

2 bulbs Trader Joe's Fresh Fennel (in the refrigerated case)

2 tablespoons olive oil

½ teaspoon garlic powder

salt and pepper

VEGAN, GLUTEN-FREE

Preheat the oven to 400°F and line a rimmed baking sheet with parchment paper. Trim the fennel bulbs, removing any green sprigs, and slice off a thin layer from the bottom. Slice into ½-inch-thick slices, top to bottom. Brush both sides of each slice with olive oil and spread out on the prepared baking sheet. Sprinkle with the garlic powder and a light dusting of salt and pepper. Roast until tender, 20 to 25 minutes.

MAKES: 4 servings

COCONUT CURRY POLENTA

Spicy, creamy polenta…there's really nothing quite like it. Serve this decadent dish as a simple side with a salad and soup.

2 tablespoons olive oil

1 tablespoon grated fresh ginger

2 teaspoons curry powder

1 cup Trader Joe's Light Coconut Milk (canned)

1 (18-ounce) log Trader Joe's Organic Polenta, crumbled

VEGAN, GLUTEN-FREE

In a small stockpot, heat the oil over medium low heat. Add the ginger and sauté until fragrant, 2 to 3 minutes. Add the curry powder and incorporate into a paste before whisking in the coconut milk. Add the polenta and whisk until smooth. Cook the polenta until creamy and heated through, 5 to 10 minutes.

MAKES: 4 servings

COOK'S NOTE: Resist the urge to add salt to this dish—the polenta has enough sodium as is!

Main Dishes

The main dish. It's the centerpiece of the meal. It's the focal point of dinnertime. It's the reason we gather. Well, that's a bit grandiose. But, at the same time, a solid entrée goes a long way. Pasta and vegetables and beans and tofu…the combinations are many and delicious.

- ROASTED CARROT RISOTTO
- BBQ BOWL
- SNAP CASHEW CRUNCH
- EASY EGGPLANT PASTA
- OLIVE MY LOVE PASTA
- MUMUSAS
- NO-NONSENSE GNOCCHI
- ORECCHIETTE WITH CREAMY TAPENADE
- TEMPEH MEATLOAF
- TEMPEH CRUMBLES
- CREAMY ARTICHOKE PASTA
- QUICK CALZONES
- TERIYAKI-GLAZED PORTOBELLOS
- EASY ASIAN STIR-FRY
- SESAME GOMASIO
- CURRIED SQUASH-ETTI
- TEMPEH TACOS
- BAKED TOFU

ROASTED CARROT RISOTTO

Risotto is not a shortcut meal; it requires low temperatures and lots of stirring...but it's worth every minute. Roasting the carrots enhances their earthy flavors and adds an intoxicating complexity of flavor. Serve with a salad and some crusty bread.

½ pound whole organic carrots

1 tablespoon olive oil

1 teaspoon balsamic vinegar

1 tablespoon unsalted butter

1 small yellow or white onion, finely diced

1 cup Trader Joe's Arborio Rice

4 cups Trader Joe's Organic Hearty Vegetable Broth

1½ cups Trader Joe's Freshly Shaved Parmesan, Romano & Asiago Cheese

salt and pepper

GLUTEN-FREE

Preheat the oven to 400°F and line a rimmed baking sheet with parchment paper. Halve the carrots lengthwise, then cut into 1-inch sticks. In a medium bowl, toss the carrots with the olive oil and vinegar and sprinkle with salt and pepper. Spread the carrots on the prepared sheet and roast until tender, 20 to 25 minutes. Remove from the oven and puree in a food processor or blender, until smooth, adding a little water 1 tablespoon at a time, if needed. In a large stockpot, melt the butter over medium low heat. Add the onion and sauté until slightly translucent, about 3 minutes. Add the rice and sauté for about 3 more minutes. Add 1 cup of the broth, reduce the heat to just a tinge above low and cook, stirring often, until absorbed. Repeat with the second and third cups of broth, 1 cup at a time. Add the carrot puree with the fourth cup of broth. Once absorbed, remove from the heat and stir in the cheese, stirring until melted and well combined.

MAKES: 4 to 6 servings

VEGAN OPTION: Replace the butter with Trader Joe's Vegan Buttery Spread. In place of the cheese, while the carrots are roasting, soak ½ cup of raw cashews in warm water. Let them soak until you are cooking the risotto. Drain the water and puree the cashews with ¼ teaspoon of salt and a squeeze of lemon juice (about ½ teaspoon). Add the cashew puree in place of the shaved cheese.

BBQ BOWL

This bowl is my standby dinner. It's tasty, filling, and makes for great leftovers. There's no better way to make your coworkers jealous than to release whiffs of barbecue sauce, rich with garlic and other delicious notes, into the office air.

2 tablespoons olive oil

1 (15-ounce) can Trader Joe's Organic Garbanzo Beans, drained and rinsed

2 tablespoons water

½ cup Trader Joe's Bold & Smoky Kansas City Style Barbecue Sauce

2 cups Very Versatile Quinoa (page 118)

Roasted Brussels Sprouts (page 110)

grated Parmesan cheese, to serve

GLUTEN-FREE

In a large sauté pan or skillet, heat the oil over medium low heat. Sauté the garbanzos until lightly browned, 3 to 5 minutes, stirring often. Add the water and barbecue sauce and sauté until the sauce thickens and coats the garbanzos and they are tender. Serve over the quinoa, on 1 side of the bowl. Spoon the brussels sprouts onto the other half of the bowl. Top with Parmesan to serve.

MAKES: 4 servings

VEGAN OPTION: Omit the Parmesan.

SNAP CASHEW CRUNCH

Sweet, salty, and a little bit spicy, this rice dish is bursting with texture and flavor. Crank up the heat or keep it low, as instructed below. This dish is flexible with the grain—use freshly cooked rice or the reliable frozen options at Joe's. Or avoid rice altogether and opt for quinoa or couscous.

3 tablespoons olive oil

¼ cup Trader Joe's Reduced Sodium Soy Sauce

1 tablespoon Trader Joe's Organic Evaporated Cane Juice Sugar

½ teaspoon cayenne pepper

1 small red onion, diced

1 (12-ounce) bag Trader Joe's Sugar Snap Peas

1 heaping cup chopped green onions, white and light-green parts only

½ cup Trader Joe's Raw Cashew Pieces

3 cups cooked rice

VEGAN

In a large sauté pan or skillet, combine the oil, soy sauce, and sugar, and heat over medium heat until bubbling and the sugar is dissolved, 3 to 4 minutes. Reduce the heat to medium low and whisk in the cayenne. Add the red onion and cook for about 1 minute. Add the peas and cover, cooking until vibrant green and slightly tender when pierced with a fork. Remove from the heat and add the green onions, cashews, and rice, tossing well to incorporate.

MAKES: 4 to 6 servings

EASY EGGPLANT PASTA

I am not typically a big lover of eggplant, but there's just something about these tender cubes of it, simmered with some tangy bruschetta, that hit the spot. Served over pasta, it makes a filling meal.

1 large eggplant

salt

3 cups Trader Joe's Organic Whole Wheat Penne Pasta

2 tablespoons olive oil

2 cups chopped white or crimini mushrooms

1 (12-ounce) jar Trader Giotto's Bruschetta

VEGAN

Cut the eggplant into 1-inch-thick slices. Sprinkle with salt and let the eggplant "sweat" in a bowl for at least 30 minutes. This removes the bitterness. Rinse off the eggplant and cut it into cubes. In a large pot, cook the pasta according to the package directions. While the pasta is cooking, heat the oil in a large sauté pan or skillet over medium heat. Add the mushrooms and the eggplant and cook until the mushrooms release their juices and darken and the eggplant is tender, about 15 minutes, stirring often. You might need to add a little water, 2 tablespoons at a time. Add the bruschetta and cook until heated through and bubbling, about 10 more minutes. Serve the eggplant mixture over the pasta.

MAKES: 4 servings

GLUTEN-FREE OPTION: Use one of Trader Joe's excellent gluten-free pastas in place of the penne.

OLIVE MY LOVE PASTA

Trader Joe's has a fantastic selection of jarred olives. High-quality and bursting with flavor, olives take center stage in this simple pasta and make a seemingly ordinary dish explode with nuance and texture.

½ pound Trader Joe's Organic Pasta Spaghetti

¼ cup good-quality olive oil

4 cloves garlic, thinly sliced

2 teaspoons dried oregano

⅛ teaspoon salt

1 cup assorted olives, coarsely chopped

½ cup grated Parmesan cheese

2 large Roma tomatoes, sliced

1 lemon, cut into 4 wedges

Italian parsley, chopped, for garnish (optional)

Cook the pasta according to the package directions. While the pasta is cooking, heat the olive oil in a large sauté pan or skillet over medium low heat. Add the garlic and cook until fragrant, about 1 minute. Add the oregano and salt. Add the olives and cook until just heated through. Toss the pasta with the olive sauce. Top servings of the pasta with Parmesan and serve with slices of tomato and a wedge of lemon to squeeze over top. Garnish with the Italian parsley, if using.

MAKES: 4 servings

VEGAN OPTION: Omit the Parmesan.

GLUTEN-FREE OPTION: Use a gluten-free pasta in place of the spaghetti.

ORECCHIETTE WITH CREAMY TAPENADE

Orecchiette has long been my favorite type of pasta. Its little domes hold creamy sauce perfectly and it has a wonderfully toothsome texture. In this recipe, it marries beautifully with the tangy, creamy tapenade sauce. Served with a green salad and some crusty bread, this simple yet luxurious pasta is sure to become a fast favorite.

2½ cups Trader Joe's Italian Orecchiette

3 tablespoons olive oil

3 cloves garlic, minced

1½ cups milk

4 ounces whole milk cream cheese

½ (9.5-ounce) jar Trader Joe's Olive Tapenade with Kalamata & Chalikidiki Olives

salt and pepper

Cook the pasta according to the package directions. In a large saucepan over low heat, heat the oil and sauté the garlic until fragrant, about 2 minutes. Add the milk and cream cheese, increase the heat to medium low and cook, whisking constantly, until the cream cheese melts and is incorporated into the milk. Whisk in the tapenade and cook until heated through. Season to taste with salt and pepper. Add the pasta to the saucepan and mix until thoroughly coated with the sauce.

MAKES: 4 servings

VEGAN OPTION: Replace the milk and cream cheese with nondairy equivalents.

GLUTEN-FREE OPTION: Use a gluten-free pasta variety in place of the orecchiette.

COOK'S NOTE: Occasionally tapenades contain anchovies. While this particular TJ's variety is fish free, brands and types may vary, so always check the label.

TEMPEH MEATLOAF

This is classic meatloaf, but without the meat. Hearty and full of flavor, a leftover slice would make for a delicious sandwich the next day. Perfect! For a grain, you can use frozen rice, a rice blend, or quinoa.

2 (8-ounce) packages Trader Joe's Organic 3 Grain Tempeh

1 cup cooked grain

1 small white or yellow onion, shredded

1 carrot, shredded

3 cloves garlic, minced

2 tablespoons red wine vinegar

2 tablespoons Trader Joe's Reduced Sodium Soy Sauce

3 tablespoons olive oil

juice and grated zest of 1 medium orange

2 teaspoons dried oregano

1 cup fresh bread crumbs

¼ cup Trader Joe's Organic Ketchup

VEGAN

Preheat the oven to 350°F and lightly grease a 9 x 5-inch loaf pan. In the bowl of a food processor or just a large bowl, crumble the packages of tempeh. Add the grain and mix. Add the shredded onion, carrot, and garlic. In a small bowl, combine the vinegar, soy sauce, olive oil, and orange juice and zest. Add the liquid to the tempeh mixture. Finally, add the oregano and bread crumbs. If you're not using the food processor, you'll probably need to use your hands to mix everything up. If processing it, pulse the mixture, scraping down the walls as needed. Spread the loaf mixture into the prepared pan and spread the ketchup over the top of it. Bake until the loaf is browned and set on the edges, about 50 minutes. Let it cool for at least 15 minutes before running a knife around the edge to loosen.

MAKES: 10 to 12 slices of meatloaf

TEMPEH CRUMBLES

These crumbles make a tasty, salty-sweet protein with a variety of uses. Sometimes it's perfect as a side, sometimes it's best with gravy, and sometimes it hits the mark served cold over a salad. You really can't go wrong. Whip up a batch and keep them in the fridge; you'll find plenty of reasons to use them.

2 tablespoons mild vegetable oil

¼ cup minced white or yellow onion

1 clove garlic, minced

1 (8-ounce) package Trader Joe's Organic 3 Grain Tempeh

2 tablespoons Trader Joe's Reduced Sodium Soy Sauce

2 tablespoons Organic Trader Joe's Organic Maple Agave Syrup Blend

2 tablespoons water

½ teaspoon Trader Joe's Toasted Sesame Oil

VEGAN

In a medium sauté pan, heat the oil over medium heat. Add the onion and cook until softened and translucent, about 5 minutes. Add the garlic and cook for 1 minute more. Crumble the tempeh in the pan. In a small bowl, whisk together the soy sauce, maple-agave syrup, water, and sesame oil before pouring it over the tempeh. Mix well and simmer until all the liquid is absorbed and the tempeh crumbles are browned, 5 to 8 minutes.

MAKES: 2 to 2¼ cups of crumbles

CREAMY ARTICHOKE PASTA

When you just need a plate of perfect carbs coated in a creamy but complex sauce, this pasta is your answer.

½ pound Trader Joe's pasta—a curly variety to catch all the yumminess

2 tablespoons olive oil

2 cloves garlic, thinly sliced

zest of 1 lemon

1 cup Trader Joe's Artichoke Antipasto

1 cup shredded mozzarella

2 tablespoons capers

salt and pepper

lemon wedges, to garnish

Cook the pasta according to the package directions. While the pasta is cooking, heat the olive oil in a large sauté pan or skillet over medium low heat. Add the garlic and cook until fragrant, about 1 minute. Add the lemon zest and artichoke antipasto, and mix to combine, cooking until warmed through. In a large bowl, toss the cooked pasta with the antipasto mixture. Add mozzarella and capers, and mix to combine until it's a cheesy, tangled mess. Add salt and pepper to taste and serve with a slice of lemon for an optional little squeeze.

MAKES: 4 large servings

QUICK CALZONES

Nothing quite hits home like a calzone. And with TJ's help, throwing them together is a breeze, so you can totally soothe yourself mid-week when you just can't muster the energy to spend much time in the kitchen. Tired? No problem, TJ's has got you covered. Consider the below a guideline—add any of your favorite pizza toppings!

1 (16-ounce) bag Trader Joe's Pizza Dough (in the refrigerated case), at room temperature

½ (14-ounce) can Trader Joe's Artichoke Hearts, drained and chopped

2 cups Trader Joe's Shredded Mozzarella Cheese

¼ cup drained, chopped Trader Joe's Pitted Kalamata Olives

1 (16-ounce) jar Trader Joe's Fat Free Pizza Sauce, warmed, to serve

Preheat the oven to 450°F and lightly dust a rimmed baking sheet with flour. Lightly dust your hands and a clean working surface with flour. Turn out the dough onto the surface and lightly knead until elastic. Divide the dough into 3 roughly equal portions. Using your hands or a rolling pin, roll out each dough mound into an oval, about 8 inches wide. Divide the artichoke hearts, cheese, and olives into 3 portions, then layer 1 portion on 1 side of the dough, pulling the empty side over to seal. You might need to moisten the edges with water to make it seal. Cut a small hole on top for venting and transfer the calzone to the prepared baking sheet. Repeat with the remaining calzones, leaving 2 inches between them on the baking sheet. Bake until golden brown and raised, about 20 minutes. Let the calzones cool for 5 minutes before serving with a side of warmed pizza sauce for dipping.

MAKES: 3 calzones

VEGAN OPTION: Omit the cheese or add a shredded vegan variety.

TERIYAKI-GLAZED PORTOBELLOS

These tender and flavorful portobellos are smoky, sweet, and salty. Enjoy over rice and vegetables, alongside mashed potatoes, or as part of a salad. In whichever circumstance, they are delicious!

¼ cup Trader Joe's Soyaki Marinade

¼ cup Trader Joe's Frozen Pineapple Tidbits, thawed

1 tablespoon olive oil

2 large portobello caps, stems removed and gills scraped out

VEGAN

Preheat the oven to 350°F and lightly grease a small baking dish. In a small food processor or blender, puree the marinade, pineapple, and oil until thick and incorporated. Place the mushrooms, cap-side down, on the prepared baking dish. Pour the marinade over them and make sure the caps are coated. Bake until the center of the caps is tender, 8 to 10 minutes. Flip the caps over and spoon any remaining sauce in the middle. Turn on the oven's broiler and broil the caps until the edges are slightly charred, 1 to 2 minutes. Let the caps cool for a few minutes and then cut into thin slices.

MAKES: 2 servings

EASY ASIAN STIR-FRY

This versatile stir-fry can be easily tweaked based on what vegetables you find at Joe's or have on hand. I recommend serving with Trader Joe's Japanese Style Fried Rice or Trader Joe's Confetti Rice. You can always add pressed tofu or crumbled tempeh to bulk up the stir-fry.

2 tablespoons canola or other mild vegetable oil

2 teaspoons Trader Joe's Toasted Sesame Oil

2 tablespoons Trader Joe's Natural Rice Vinegar

1 tablespoon Trader Joe's Organic Evaporated Cane Juice Sugar

2 tablespoons lime juice

1 (16 to 18-ounce) container Trader Joe's Asian Stir Fry Vegetables (in the refrigerated case)

2 cups cooked rice

Sesame Gomasio (recipe follows), for garnish

VEGAN

In a large sauté pan or skillet, heat the canola or other mild vegetable oil over medium heat. Tilt the pan to coat with the oil, then add the sesame oil, rice vinegar, sugar, and lime juice. Mix to combine, then reduce the heat to medium low and add the vegetables. Stir to coat and then cover the vegetables with a lid and let them steam until tender, 10 to 15 minutes, stirring occasionally. While the vegetables are cooking, prepare the rice, according to the package directions. Serve the stir-fry over the rice. Garnish with the gomasio.

MAKES: 4 servings

SESAME GOMASIO

This tasty combination of seaweed and sesame is a popular topping in Japanese cuisine. My take adds a little special somethin' in the form of dried rosemary. It's delicious sprinkled on top of Japanese dishes, but I actually love it on top of popcorn. To ramp it up, use the TJ's Wasabi Roasted Seaweed Snack.

5 sheets Trader Joe's Roasted Seaweed Snack

½ teaspoon dried rosemary

3 tablespoons sesame seeds

VEGAN

In a small bowl, crush the seaweed and rosemary. If you have a spice grinder, you can make a finer grind, but coarse is good, too. Add the sesame seeds. Store the gomasio in an airtight container for up to 3 weeks.

MAKES: ½ cup of gomasio

CURRIED SQUASH-ETTI

Butternut squash has the perfect palette to showcase the flavors of curry, and it makes for a thick, rich sauce that sticks to the spaghetti beautifully. If you can, make the sauce the day before serving, to give the spices time to develop. Try serving with a side of Cucumber Raita (page 148) and cucumber slices. Trader Joe's also carries excellent jarred chutney as well.

1 small butternut squash

2 tablespoons olive oil, divided

water, as needed

½ small yellow onion, coarsely chopped

2 cloves garlic, minced

1 tablespoon curry powder

1 cup Trader Joe's Light Coconut Milk (canned)

1 (13.25-ounce) box Trader Joe's Spaghetti

VEGAN

Preheat the oven to 400°F and line a rimmed baking sheet with parchment paper. Cut the squash in half lengthwise and scoop out the seeds. Lightly brush the cut part with 1 tablespoon of the oil and place cut-side down on the prepared baking sheet. Roast until the entire squash is very tender when pierced with a fork, 1 to 1½ hours. Let the squash cool before handling. Boil a pot of water for the spaghetti and cook according to the package directions. While the pasta is cooking, heat the remaining 1 tablespoon oil in a medium saucepan over medium heat. Add the onion and cook until translucent, about 5 minutes. Add the garlic and cook for 2 more minutes. Add the curry powder and mix until the onion mixture is coated, then whisk in the coconut milk.

Scoop out the flesh of the squash into the bowl of a food processor or blender, and add the coconut milk mixture. Add water as needed and puree to make a thick sauce. Combine the sauce with the drained pasta.

MAKES: 5 to 6 servings

GLUTEN-FREE OPTION: Use a gluten-free pasta in place of the spaghetti.

MUMUSAS

Pupusas *are a sort of bean-filled tortilla. They are delicious, but very time-consuming to make. I took the basic concept and ran with it, creating these refried bean–filled cornbread muffins, which are simple and extremely tasty! Serve with salsa, guac, and a salad and call it a meal. If you're weird like me, the opportunity to use a cookie scoop with refried beans is a total highlight.*

1 cup milk

½ teaspoon mild vinegar

⅓ cup mild oil

1 (15-ounce) box Trader Joe's Cornbread Mix

1 (16-ounce) can Trader Joe's Refried Black Beans

Optional toppings: guacamole, salsa

Preheat the oven to 375°F and lightly grease and flour the cups of a standard 12-cup muffin tin. In a large bowl, whisk together the milk and vinegar, and let sit for several minutes. Add the oil and whisk. In 2 batches, add the cornbread mix until just combined. Fill each muffin cup a third of the way up with the cornbread batter. Using a cookie scoop or tablespoon, place 1 scoop of the beans in the middle of each muffin cup. Top with remaining batter until each cup is full. Bake until the tops are browned and set, 23 to 25 minutes. Let the mumusas cool in the pan, on a rack, for at least 15 minutes. Run a knife around the inside of each cup to loosen, then invert. Serve with a salad and delicious toppings like guacamole and salsa.

MAKES: 12 mumusas

COOK'S NOTE: You'll have some leftover refried beans; mix them with a can of Trader Joe's Fire Roasted Diced Green Chiles and serve as a side or dip with chips.

NO-NONSENSE GNOCCHI

These gnocchi mean business. This recipe comes together in a pinch and makes for a delicious and impressive meal with pantry and fridge basics. TJ's typically carries multiple types of gnocchi, some of which are vegan, so read the labels and get cookin'!

1 (1.1-pound) package vacuum sealed dried gnocchi

4 tablespoons olive oil

6 to 7 cloves garlic, coarsely chopped

1 tablespoon dried basil

¼ cup drained and chopped Trader Joe's Julienne Sliced Sun Dried Tomatoes in Olive Oil

3 Roma tomatoes, cored and chopped

Bring a large pot of water to a boil for the gnocchi over medium high heat. Cook the gnocchi according to the package directions, being careful to not overcook. In a large sauté pan, heat 2 tablespoons of the oil over medium heat, then add the garlic and sauté until fragrant and slightly softened, about 3 minutes. Add the basil and mix. Add the sun-dried and fresh tomatoes and stir to combine. Add the gnocchi to the pan and the remaining oil and stir to combine well. Cook the gnocchi in the tomato mixture until some of the edges begin to brown, 8 to 10 minutes, stirring often.

MAKES: 2 large or 4 smaller servings

VEGAN OPTION: The brands of gnocchi at Joe's vary by region, so be sure to read the label to ensure the gnocchi are vegan.

TEMPEH TACOS

These tacos come together quickly and make a protein-packed and flavorful meal that will satisfy herbivores and omnivores alike. You can easily substitute the tempeh with 8 ounces of well-pressed, cubed firm tofu. Beware, there's a little kick to these Mexican-inspired morsels. Refreshing guacamole is a nice complement to the spice.

2 tablespoons olive oil

½ medium yellow onion, diced

1 (8-ounce) package Trader Joe's Organic 3 Grain Tempeh

1 (14.5-ounce) can Trader Joe's Organic Tomatoes Diced & Fire Roasted with Organic Green Chiles

1 (1.3-ounce) packet Trader Joe's Taco Seasoning Mix

1 (5.5-ounce) box Trader Joe's Taco Shells, tortillas, or tortilla chips

Optional toppings: guacamole, salsa, sour cream, cilantro

VEGAN

In a large sauté pan, heat the oil over medium heat. Sauté the onions until translucent, 5 to 7 minutes. Crumble the tempeh into the onions. Add the can of tomatoes, including their juices, and the taco seasoning. Simmer until the liquid is absorbed and the mixture is thick. While the mixture is simmering, to toast the taco shells, if desired, arrange the shells on a rimmed baking sheet and bake for 3 to 5 minutes. Serve with the toasted taco shells, tortillas, or tortilla chips, and the toppings of your choice.

MAKES: 4 servings (7 or 8 tacos)

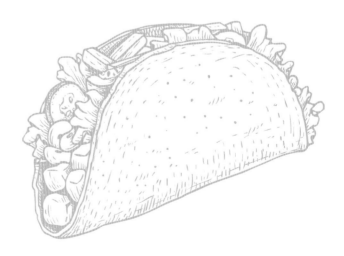

BAKED TOFU

This is my go-to tofu recipe; the flavors are amazing, so this dish is a great way to introduce tofu to newbies. It's flavorful, firm, and very versatile. It really doesn't get any better than that.

1 (14-ounce) block Trader Joe's Firm Tofu

3 cloves garlic, minced

2 tablespoons Trader Joe's Reduced Sodium Soy Sauce

2 tablespoons water

1 tablespoon olive oil

1 tablespoon red wine vinegar

1 tablespoon dried basil

1 teaspoon Trader Joe's Toasted Sesame Oil

VEGAN

Drain and press the tofu for at least 30 minutes to drain the water. Preheat the oven to 375°F. Combine the garlic, soy sauce, water, oil, vinegar, basil, and sesame oil in the bottom of a 9 x 13-inch baking pan. Cut the tofu into 8 equal slices. Dip the slices in the marinade and flip to coat. Bake until the marinade is absorbed, about 45 minutes, flipping the tofu every 15 minutes. Let the tofu cool for 10 minutes before serving and be sure to scoop up the yummy garlicky bits from the pan.

MAKES: 8 slices

GLUTEN-FREE OPTION: Replace the soy sauce with gluten-free tamari.

Casseroles

I'm from the Midwest, so I suppose I should call this chapter "Hot Dishes" but it just doesn't flow very well. It also fails to represent the breadth of recipes here: breakfast, side dishes, and entrées are united in their shared home of the casserole dish. So grab those pans and plan a potluck!

- EAST-MEETS-MIDWEST BREAKFAST BAKE
- SPRING VEGETABLE BAKE
- CUCUMBER RAITA
- SPAGHETTI AND MEATBALL BAKE
- FANCY MACARONI BAKE
- CLASSIC POT PIE
- LEEKY ONION BISCUIT BAKE
- MEXI-BAKE CASSEROLE
- CINNAMON TOAST BAKE
- ROOT OF THE EARTH CASSEROLE
- VEGAN BISCUITS
- WORKNIGHT SHEPHERD'S PIE
- SMASHING VEGAN MASHED POTATOES
- TATER TOT HOT DISH
- VERY VEGGIE LASAGNA

EAST-MEETS-MIDWEST BREAKFAST BAKE

This breakfast bake marries rich, flavorful curry with a Midwestern staple—hash browns. Essentially a giant pan of tofu scramble, this bake is perfect for popping in the oven while downing a couple of cups of coffee and trying to wake up. Serve with a Mango Lassi (page 200) on the side.

¼ cup olive oil, divided

1 medium yellow or white onion, diced

2 cloves garlic

1 large orange or red bell pepper, diced

2 tablespoons curry powder

1 (14-ounce) block Trader Joe's Firm Tofu, drained but not pressed

¾ cup Trader Joe's Light Coconut Milk (canned)

1 (6.5-ounce) bag Trader Joe's Shredded Hash browns (in the frozen section)

⅓ cup chopped fresh cilantro

salt and pepper

2¼ cups Cucumber Raita (page 148), to serve

VEGAN, GLUTEN-FREE

Preheat the oven to 375°F. Lightly grease a 9 x 13-inch baking dish. In a large sauté pan or skillet, heat 2 tablespoons of the oil over medium heat. Add the onion and cook until translucent, 3 to 4 minutes. Add the garlic and cook until fragrant, about 1 minute. Add the bell pepper and cook until the bell pepper begins to "sweat," about 2 minutes. Add the curry powder, and season with salt and pepper to taste. Remove from the heat. Crumble the tofu over the curry mixture, and add the coconut milk. Stir to combine, mashing with a potato masher for a smoother consistency. Reserve 1½ cups of the hash browns. Add the remaining frozen hash browns and cilantro and stir until well distributed. Spread the hash brown mixture in the prepared dish and top with the reserved hash browns. Brush the remaining 2 tablespoons oil over the top and cover with aluminum foil. Bake for 45 minutes before removing foil, then bake for 15 minutes more. Serve with the cucumber raita.

MAKES: 6 to 8 servings

SPRING VEGETABLE BAKE

Bright and light, this vegetable bake showcases the natural flavors of red onion, zucchini, and tomato and sprinkles them with a lovely, crunchy bread crumb and cheese topping. It's a nice, light alternative to heavier casseroles.

2 large red onions

3 large beefsteak tomatoes

2 large zucchini

2 tablespoons olive oil

½ cup Trader Joe's Japanese Style Panko Breadcrumbs

½ cup Trader Joe's Grana Padano Parmesan

salt and pepper

Preheat the oven to 375°F and lightly grease an 8-inch square baking dish. Slice the red onions and tomatoes each into ½-inch slices. Slice the zucchini at an angle to make ½-inch-wide coins. Alternate the slices in the bottom of the prepared pan, making 3 overlapping rows of vegetables. Drizzle the olive oil over the top and sprinkle with salt and pepper. In a small bowl, combine the bread crumbs and Parmesan and set aside.

Bake the vegetables for 25 minutes, then top the bake with the bread crumb topping. Bake until the bread crumbs are lightly browned and the vegetables are tender when pierced with a fork, about 10 minutes longer.

MAKES: 6 to 9 servings

VEGAN OPTION: Omit the Parmesan and double the bread crumbs.

CUCUMBER RAITA

This gentle raita offsets the spiciness of the curry in the East-Meets-Midwest Breakfast Bake (page 145). The addition of cucumbers makes this a tasty topping that you could also try with other spicy fare, like the Mexi-Bake Casserole (page 154).

1 cup peeled and shredded cucumber

½ cup peeled and chopped cucumber

2 cups plain Trader Joe's Yogurt

½ teaspoon ground cumin

sprinkle of salt

2 tablespoons chopped fresh cilantro (optional)

GLUTEN-FREE

Blot the shredded cucumber with a paper towel to reduce the juiciness. In a medium bowl combine the shredded cucumber, chopped cucumber, and yogurt, and stir until well incorporated. Add the cumin and salt and mix. Top with cilantro, if using, just before serving.

MAKES: 2¼ cups

....

VEGAN OPTION: Replace the yogurt with an unsweetened nondairy version or with a nondairy sour cream.

....

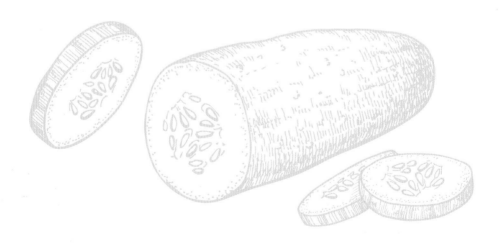

SPAGHETTI AND MEATBALL BAKE

This spaghetti casserole will forever change the way you approach marinara, pasta, and meatballs. And the bonus is it's so easy to make! If you're a sauce hound (like me), you might want to top the bake with additional sauce when it's done.

1 (16-ounce) bag Trader Joe's Organic Brown Rice Pasta, spaghetti, fusilli, or penne

1 (25-ounce) jar Trader Joe's Organic Tomato Basil Marinara

1 (16-ounce) bag Trader Joe's Meatless Meatballs (in the frozen section)

1½ cups Trader Joe's Shredded Mozzarella Cheese

Preheat the oven to 350°F and lightly grease a 9 x 13-inch baking dish. Bring a large pot of water to a boil over high heat. Cook the pasta until just tender, then drain and rinse in cool water to stop the cooking. In the prepared dish, combine the marinara, pasta, meatballs, and mozzarella, and stir until everything is incorporated. Cover with aluminum foil and bake for 20 minutes, then remove the foil and bake until the sauce is lightly bubbling, the cheese is melted, and the pasta seems set, about 10 minutes. Let cool for 15 minutes before serving.

MAKES: 6 to 8 servings

VEGAN OPTION: Omit the mozzarella or substitute with a nondairy equivalent.

FANCY MACARONI BAKE

Real mac 'n' cheese, the good stuff, requires a little elbow grease. But the steps are so easy, and the end result is so tasty, that you won't mind the work—I swear. The layer of tomatoes on the bottom of the bake adds a bit of brightness and tang to the sweet and creamy mix. Perfection.

1 tablespoon olive oil

1 small white or yellow onion, minced

1 (28-ounce) can Trader Joe's Organic Tomatoes Diced in Tomato Juice, drained

1 (16-ounce) bag Trader Joe's Italian Rigatoni

3 tablespoons unsalted butter

¼ cup unbleached all-purpose flour

3 cups milk

2 teaspoons Dijon mustard

1 teaspoon garlic powder

½ teaspoon salt

4 cups Trader Joe's 3 Cheese Blend, divided

1½ cups Trader Joe's Freshly Shaved Parmesan, Romano & Asiago Cheese

2 cups Trader Joe's Japanese Style Panko Breadcrumbs

Preheat the oven to 375°F and lightly grease a 9 x 11-inch casserole dish. In a medium sauté pan or skillet, heat the oil over medium heat. Add the onion and sauté until translucent, 3 to 5 minutes. Add the tomatoes and stir to incorporate. Pour the tomato mixture into the bottom of the prepared casserole dish and set aside. Bring a large stockpot of water to a boil. Cook the pasta according to the package directions while you start to make the cheese sauce. If the pasta is done before the sauce, simply drain and set aside.

To make the cheese sauce, melt the butter in a large pot over medium heat. Whisk in the flour and cook until lightly browned and fragrant, about 2 minutes, whisking constantly. Starting with ½ cup of the milk, whisk the milk into the flour mixture, incorporating it until smooth. Add the mustard, garlic powder, and salt. Reduce the heat to low and cook until it begins to slightly bubble, being careful not to boil. Remove from the heat and whisk in 3 cups of the 3-cheese blend and the Parmesan. Add the cooked pasta to the cheese sauce and mix to combine. Spread the noodle mixture over top of the tomatoes. Sprinkle the remaining 1 cup of the cheese blend and the bread crumbs over the top. Bake for 20 to 25 minutes, until the cheese is bubbling on the edges and the bread crumbs are lightly browned.

MAKES: 8 to 10 servings

VEGAN OPTION: Replace the butter with Trader Joe's Vegan Buttery Spread. In place of the cheese sauce, blend 1 (14-ounce) block Trader Joe's Organic Firm Tofu with 1 cup Trader Joe's Tahini Sauce (in the refrigerated case), 2 cups unsweetened nondairy milk, 2 teaspoons lemon juice, and ¼ teaspoon sea salt. Reserve ¾ cup of the sauce and incorporate the rest with the cooked noodles. Pour the remaining sauce on top, along with the bread crumbs. Alternatively, you could replace the cheese blend, Parmesan, and milk with a blend of vegan cheeses and unsweetened nondairy milk.

CLASSIC POT PIE

If you're really craving a pot pie like Grandma used to make, Trader Joe's sells packages of Chicken-less Strips, which you could add to get that home-cooked chicken taste, but I prefer to keep it mellow with white kidney beans.

2 tablespoons olive oil

1 small white or yellow onion, diced

2 cloves garlic, minced

2 teaspoons dried thyme

2 tablespoons dried basil

2 small carrots, scrubbed and cut into ¼-inch-thick coins

1 red bell pepper, diced

1 medium potato, peeled and cut into a ½-inch dice

1 teaspoon salt

1 (14-ounce) can Trader Joe's White Kidney Beans, drained and rinsed

½ cup Trader Joe's Petite Peas (in the frozen section)

1 cup water

1 tablespoon unbleached all-purpose flour

1 cup shredded cheddar cheese

1 sheet Trader Joe's Artisan Puff Pastry (in the frozen section)

1 tablespoon melted unsalted butter

Preheat the oven to 350°F and lightly grease an 8-inch square casserole dish or a deep 8-inch pie pan. In a large sauté pan, heat the oil over medium heat. Add the onion and cook until translucent, about 5 minutes. Add the garlic and sauté until fragrant, about 2 minutes. Add the thyme and basil and stir to coat the onions. Mix in the carrots, bell pepper, and potato; sprinkle with the salt. Reduce the heat to medium low and cook, covered, stirring often, until the potatoes and carrots are slightly softened, 10 to 15 minutes. You might need to add a splash of water occasionally to deglaze the pan. Add the kidney beans and the peas. In a small bowl, whisk together the water and flour. Pour over the vegetable mix and increase the heat to medium. Bring the sauce to a boil, then lower the heat to low and simmer until the sauce starts to thicken, about 5 minutes.

Pour the vegetable mixture into the prepared casserole dish. Sprinkle the cheese on top. Cover the dish with the puff pastry, pressing it down firmly around the edges and trimming any excess as needed. Cut a vent in the middle of the pot pie and then brush the top with the melted butter. Bake until the pastry is puffed and golden, 40 to 45 minutes. Let the pot pie cool for 15 minutes to set up before slicing and serving.

MAKES: 4 to 5 large servings

VEGAN OPTION: Omit the cheese and replace the TJ's puff pastry with a vegan version and the butter with Trader Joe's Vegan Buttery Spread.

VARIATION: Make 4 individual pies by using ramekins. Cut the puff pastry into 4 squares and follow as directed above.

LEEKY ONION BISCUIT BAKE

This casserole is total comfort food: warm vegetables and creamy beans smothered with sauce and topped with flaky biscuits. It really doesn't get better than that. If you have an ovenproof sauté pan or skillet or a cast-iron pan that you can make this in, simply top the skillet contents with the biscuits and transfer to the oven.

2 tablespoons olive oil

2 cups sliced mushrooms

1 medium sweet onion, chopped

1 package of leeks, dark leaves removed, rinsed and chopped to ¼-inch-thick half moons)

1 tablespoon dried basil

1 tablespoon fresh thyme

½ teaspoon salt

1 (15-ounce) can Trader Joe's White Kidney Beans, rinsed and drained

½ cup water

2 tablespoons unbleached all-purpose flour

1 (16-ounce) canister Trader Joe's Buttermilk Biscuits

Preheat the oven to 350°F and lightly grease an 8-inch square casserole dish. In a large sauté pan or skillet, heat the oil over medium heat. Sauté the onions and leeks, stirring often, until sweating and slightly softened, about 5 minutes. Add the mushrooms and cook until softened and the juices release, about 5 minutes. Add the basil, thyme, and salt and stir to combine. Stir in the onions, leeks, and white kidney beans and lower the heat to medium low. Place a lid on the skillet and cook until everything is heated through, about 15 minutes, stirring often. You may need to add a little water to loosen up any brown bits on the bottom of the skillet.

In a small bowl, whisk together the water and flour. Pour over the vegetable mixture and increase the heat to medium. Cook until the liquid begins to bubble, about 5 minutes. Transfer the sauté pan or skillet contents to the prepared casserole dish and top with the biscuits, placing them about 1 inch apart. Bake until the biscuits are puffy and golden brown and the liquid is bubbling around the edges, 15 to 20 minutes. Let the casserole cool for 5 minutes before serving.

MAKES: 8 servings

VEGAN OPTION: Top with 6 Vegan Biscuits (page 159).

MEXI-BAKE CASSEROLE

Sweet cornbread, spicy soy chorizo, and tender black beans come together in this tasty casserole that will become a staple dish for your family. This recipe was a big hit with testers—one them even e-mailed later to say that her omnivorous husband took leftovers to work and was bombarded with requests for the recipe based on smell alone. I'd say that's quite the testament!

½ teaspoon garlic powder

⅓ cup mild vegetable oil

1 cup milk

½ teaspoon mild vinegar

1 (15-ounce) box Trader Joe's Cornbread Mix

1½ cups Trader Joe's Shredded 3 Cheese Blend, divided

1 (15-ounce) can Trader Joe's Organic Black Beans, drained and rinsed

1 (12-ounce) package Trader Joe's Soy Chorizo, crumbled into large chunks

1 tablespoon olive oil

2 large onions, sliced into half-moons

2 large bell peppers, sliced

Optional toppings: salsa, guacamole, sour cream

Preheat the oven to 350°F and lightly grease an 8 x 11-inch baking dish. In a large bowl, whisk together the garlic powder, vegetable oil, milk, and vinegar. Incorporate the cornbread mix into the wet ingredients. Mix in half of the cheese. Sprinkle half of the beans and half of the chorizo in the bottom of the baking dish. Spread the cornbread mixture over the chorizo and top with the remaining beans and chorizo. Draw a knife through the mixture several times to incorporate. Top with the remaining cheese. Bake until a toothpick inserted into the center comes out clean, 35 to 40 minutes. Let rest for 10 minutes before serving.

While the casserole is baking, heat the olive oil in a large sauté pan or skillet over medium heat. Sauté the onions and peppers until tender but still crisp, about 5 minutes. Serve slices of the bake on top of the sautéed onions and peppers, with whatever toppings you desire.

MAKES: 9 to 12 slices

VEGAN OPTION: Omit the cheese or replace with a nondairy equivalent.

CINNAMON TOAST BAKE

Oh my. If you like French toast, this recipe is for you. Or, if you like cinnamon-packed cereal, this recipe is for you. In fact, I can't think of anyone who wouldn't like this tasty brunch bake. Put it together the night before and you can just pop it in the oven when you wake up. Voilà—breakfast is served!

Trader Joe's has some amazing bread varieties to pick from that are excellent for this recipe. I tend to go with the more rustic Italian breads, but you could use a fresh baguette or opt for challah for complete decadence. Serve it with maple-agave syrup or with yogurt and fresh fruit.

10 large (1-inch-thick) slices of bread

1⅓ cups milk

4 eggs

1½ cups Greek-style yogurt

2 tablespoons Trader Joe's Organic Maple Agave Syrup Blend

1½ teaspoons vanilla extract

1 tablespoon plus ½ teaspoon ground cinnamon, divided

¼ cup Trader Joe's Organic Evaporated Cane Juice Sugar

Optional toppings: yogurt, maple-agave-syrup, fruit

Lightly grease an 8 x 11-inch casserole dish. Layer the bottom with 1 solid layer of bread slices, tearing the bread to fill in cracks as needed. In a large bowl, whisk together the milk, eggs, yogurt, maple-agave syrup, vanilla, and ½ teaspoon of the cinnamon. Pour half of the mixture over the bread layer in the casserole. Add the second layer of bread and top with the remaining milk mixture. Cover the pan with plastic wrap and refrigerate for at least 2 hours, preferably overnight.

Preheat the oven to 375°F. Remove the plastic wrap from the dish. In a small bowl, combine the remaining 1 tablespoon cinnamon and the sugar. Sprinkle the mixture over the top of the bake. Bake for 30 minutes, until the top is set and a knife inserted into the center comes out clean. Let the bake rest for 10 minutes before serving.

MAKES: 6 to 8 servings

VEGAN OPTION: Use nondairy milk, nondairy yogurt, and vegan bread. In place of the eggs, puree ⅔ cup of tofu with ¼ cup nondairy milk and 1 teaspoon cornstarch.

ROOT OF THE EARTH CASSEROLE

Comfort food. Hearty, earthy vegetables marry with cream cheese and vegetable broth in this recipe, creating a rich and satisfying casserole that would be delicious alongside soup and a salad on a chilly day.

1 tablespoon olive oil, plus more for brushing

1 small white or yellow onion, diced

1 tablespoon dried basil

2 stems celery, cut to ½-inch slices

2 leeks, white and light-green parts only, washed and sliced to ½-inch slices

1½ cups Trader Joe's Artichoke Hearts (in the frozen section)

8 ounces cream cheese

1 cup Trader Joe's Organic Hearty Vegetable Broth

2 russet potatoes, cut into ¼-inch slices

salt and pepper

GLUTEN-FREE

Preheat the oven to 400°F and lightly grease an 8-inch square baking dish. In a large sauté pan or skillet, heat 1 tablespoon of the olive oil on medium heat. Add the onion and cook until translucent, about 3 minutes. Add the basil, celery, leeks, artichokes, and salt and pepper to taste, and stir to coat. Chop the cream cheese into chunks and add to the pan. Add the vegetable broth and simmer, stirring often, until the cream cheese melts into the broth and the vegetables are slightly tender.

Spread the creamy vegetable mixture in the bottom of the prepared dish. Lay the potato slices in a single overlapping layer on top. Lightly brush the top with olive oil. Bake until the potatoes are tender and lightly browned and the casserole is lightly bubbling on the edges, 38 to 42 minutes.

MAKES: 6 to 9 servings

VEGAN OPTION: Use Trader Joe's Vegan Cream Cheese Alternative in place of the dairy cream cheese.

VEGAN BISCUITS

These biscuits are so tender and moist, no one will ever know they're vegan. It doesn't hurt that they come together so quickly, too.

1 cup unbleached all-purpose flour

1 cup white whole wheat flour

2 teaspoons baking powder

1 teaspoon baking soda

¼ teaspoon salt

¾ cup nondairy milk

1 teaspoon mild vinegar

¼ cup oil

VEGAN

Preheat the oven to 425°F and line a rimmed baking sheet with parchment paper. In a large bowl, combine the all-purpose flour, white whole wheat flour, and baking powder, baking soda, and salt. In a medium bowl, mix the milk and vinegar. Let sit for 2 minutes. Add the oil and whisk quickly. Add the wet ingredients to the dry ingredients and mix until just combined, being sure to scrape the bottom of the bowl. The dough may be slightly lumpy.

If using for the Leeky Onion Biscuit Bake (page 153) use the biscuit dough on top of the casserole, or proceed to make the biscuits on their own. Drop 6 large scoops of the dough on the baking sheet, at least 3 inches apart. Bake until puffy and browned, about 10 minutes. Store leftover biscuits covered at room temperature.

MAKES: 6 biscuits

WORKNIGHT SHEPHERD'S PIE

This recipe comes together quickly and is hearty and comforting—perfect for dreary winter nights. Serve with a nice crusty bread.

½ (16-ounce) bag Trader Joe's Green Beans (in the frozen section), chopped and thawed

½ (16-ounce) bag Trader Joe's Colorful Carrot Coins (in the frozen section), thawed

2 (17-ounce) aseptic containers of Trader Joe's Organic Lentil Vegetable Soup, drained

½ (28-ounce) bag Trader Joe's Mashed Potatoes (in the frozen section), thawed

Preheat the oven to 375°F and lightly grease an 8-inch square casserole dish. In a large bowl, combine the beans, carrots, and lentil soup. Spread the mixture into the prepared casserole dish and top with a layer of mashed potatoes. Cover with aluminum foil and bake for 40 minutes. Remove the aluminum foil and bake until the potatoes are lightly golden and the lentil mixture is bubbling along the edges of the dish, about 15 minutes. Remove from the oven and let cool for 10 minutes before serving.

MAKES: 5 to 6 servings

VEGAN OPTION: Use a 20-ounce container of Trader Joe's Lentil Soup with Ancient Grains (in the refrigerated case), undrained, and top with Smashing Vegan Mashed Potatoes (recipe follows).

SMASHING VEGAN MASHED POTATOES

This recipe is creamy, comforting, and vegan. Now, there's a combo! You can dress it up with fresh chives or more garlic. I leave a little skin on the potatoes for the extra color and more texture, but if you're using nonorganic potatoes, I recommend peeling them entirely.

2 pounds yellow or red potatoes, skins mostly peeled, cut into 1-inch cubes

3 tablespoons Trader Joe's Vegan Buttery Spread

2 tablespoons Trader Joe's Vegan Cream Cheese Alternative

3 to 4 tablespoons nondairy milk, as needed

2 cloves garlic, minced

salt and pepper

VEGAN

In a medium pot, cover the potatoes with water, by about 1 inch. Bring to a simmer over medium high heat and cook until the potatoes are tender when pierced with a fork, 15 to 20 minutes. Drain the potatoes and place back in the pot, off the heat. Add the spread, cream cheese alternative, 3 tablespoons nondairy milk, and garlic. Mash the potatoes with a potato masher, incorporating the other ingredients until creamy. Add more nondairy milk if needed. Season to taste with salt and pepper.

MAKES: 4 to 6 servings

TATER TOT HOT DISH

What kind of Midwesterner would I be if I didn't include a tater tot hot dish recipe? It's practically an emblem on the Minnesota state flag (implemented properly, a giant mosquito wearing a Vikings helmet would be draining the hot dish). But really, nothing provides as much comfort as a warm, creamy plate of tater tot hot dish.

2 tablespoons olive oil

1 small white or yellow onion, diced

2 cloves garlic, minced

2 (12-ounce) packages Trader Joe's Beef-less Ground Beef

1 recipe Souper Easy Mushroom Soup (page 89)

½ (2-pound) bag Trader Joe's Trader Potato Tots (in the frozen section), thawed

VEGAN

Preheat the oven to 350°F and lightly grease a 9 x 13-inch casserole dish. In a large sauté pan or skillet, heat the oil over medium heat. Add the onion and cook until translucent, about 5 minutes. Add the garlic and cook until fragrant, about 2 minutes. Mix in the "beef" and cook just until heated through. Add the mushroom soup and mix well. Spread the mushroom mixture on the bottom of the prepared casserole dish and top with a solid layer of tots. Bake until the tots are golden and the casserole is bubbling, 45 to 60 minutes. Let cool for 15 minutes before serving

MAKES: 6 to 8 servings

VERY VEGGIE LASAGNA

Half lasagna noodles, half vegetables, filled with a rich and creamy tofu ricotta, this lasagna gives you all of the comfort of a slab of lasagna while being chock-full of vegetables.

TOFU RICOTTA:

1 container <u>Trader Joe's Firm Tofu</u>

¼ cup tahini

2 to 4 tablespoons olive oil

2 to 3 cloves garlic

¼ cup Trader Joe's Nutritional Yeast

1 to 2 tablespoons fresh lemon juice

2 teaspoons dried basil

1 teaspoon dried oregano

½ teaspoon salt

¼ cup water

PASTA AND VEGGIES:

1 (25-ounce) jar Trader Joe's Organic Tomato Basil Marinara

¼ cup water

1 (16-ounce) box Trader Joe's Italian No Boil Lasagna Noodles

2 large zucchini or yellow squash, trimmed and sliced lengthwise into ¼-inch-thick slices

2 cups shredded mozzarella cheese (optional)

Place all of the ricotta ingredients into a food processor and blend until smooth. Add a little water if needed—it should be spreadable but not too thin.

Preheat the oven to 375°F. In a bowl, whisk together the marinara and water. To the bottom of a 9 x 13-inch pan, add about ½ cup of the marinara, 3 to 4 of the lasagna noodles (slightly overlapping), and ¼ of the tofu ricotta mixture. Add 1 layer of zucchini noodles, then another ½ cup of the marinara and the tofu ricotta. Repeat another set of layers: lasagna noodles, marinara, tofu ricotta, zucchini, tofu ricotta, and marinara, and end with a layer of lasagna noodles and marinara. Cover with foil and bake for 35 minutes. Remove the foil and top with the mozzarella, then return to the oven for 15 to 20 more minutes, until the cheese is browned and edges of the lasagna are bubbling and bronzed. Let sit at room temperature for 20 minutes before slicing and serving.

MAKES: 6 large servings

Desserts

All right, here's the good stuff. Everyone likes a good meal, but everyone *loves* a good dessert. So roll up your sleeves, dig in, and prepare to make the world a tastier place.

- EARL OF ORANGE CAKE
- BANANAS FOR GLUTEN-FREE BROWNIES
- I'M SO MAD ABOUT 'STACHIOS COOKIES
- HASTY PASTIES
- VEGAN PIE CRUST
- QUICK KHEER
- PAPPY'S PISTACHIO PUDDING
- FALL PUMPKIN SPICE COBBLER
- GINGERED BREAD PUDDING
- AMAZING EVERYTHING COOKIES
- BEST CHEESECAKE
- BEST VEGAN CHEESECAKE
- CHEWY MOCHA ICE CREAM CAKE
- HOMEMADE DULCE DE LECHE
- CASHEW NIBBLE COOKIES
- BACK-IN-THE-DAY DATE BARS
- APPLE UPSIDE-DOWN CAKE
- FRUITY BROWN, BUTTERED CRISPY TREATS
- PARSNIP CAKE WITH BROWNED BUTTER CREAM CHEESE FROSTING
- BROWNED BUTTER CREAM CHEESE FROSTING
- EASY FRUIT AND CHEESECAKE GALETTE
- TAHINI-DOODLES
- FIG DELIGHT
- SCOUT'S HONOR MACAROONS

EARL OF ORANGE CAKE

This snack cake is tender, moist, and infused with orange and earthy Earl Grey goodness. It's perfect for a light dessert or midday snack with a cuppa. It's sweet and delicious on its own, but the glaze really ramps up the orange.

CAKE:

2 cups milk

6 Trader Joe's Earl Grey Tea bags

2 cups unbleached all-purpose flour

⅔ cup Trader Joe's Organic Evaporated Cane Juice Sugar

2 teaspoons baking powder

¼ teaspoon salt

¼ cup mild vegetable oil

½ teaspoon vanilla extract

¼ teaspoon mild vinegar

2 (11-ounce) cans Trader Joe's Mandarin Oranges, drained

GLAZE (OPTIONAL):

1 tablespoon orange juice

1 tablespoon grated orange zest

½ to ¾ cup Trader Joe's Organic Powdered Sugar, sifted

To make the cake: Preheat the oven to 375°F. Line the bottom of an 8-inch square baking pan with parchment or lightly grease and flour an 8-inch baking pan (round or square). Pour the nondairy milk into a small saucepan. Add the tea bags and bring to a simmer over medium heat. Simmer for 3 to 5 minutes, being mindful that it doesn't boil. Remove from the heat and let the tea steep until the milk cools. Squeeze out the tea bags, then open the bags and measure out 2 teaspoons of the steeped tea leaves, and set aside; diskard the tea bags and remaining leaves. Stir together the flour, sugar, baking powder, and salt. In a large bowl, combine the tea-steeped milk, oil, steeped tea leaves, vanilla, and vinegar. Incorporate the dry ingredients into the wet ingredients in 2 batches, mixing until just incorporated. Arrange the mandarin sections in the bottom of the prepared pan. Spread the batter over the top and bake until a toothpick inserted in the center comes out clean, 35 to 40 minutes. Let the cake cool in the pan on a cooling rack.

To make the glaze, if using: In a small bowl, whisk together the orange juice, zest, and powdered sugar, adding just enough sugar to make a thick but pourable glaze. Spread it over the top of the warm cake. Let the cake finish cooling before serving.

MAKES: 9 to 12 slices

VEGAN OPTION: Substitute the milk with a nondairy equivalent.

BANANAS FOR GLUTEN-FREE BROWNIES

These brownies have banana coming at you in three ways: mashed in the batter, flattened into a fudgy center, and sprinkled on top for crunchy banana chip bites. The combination makes for a rich and fudgy 'nana brownie that everyone—vegan, gluten-intolerant, and otherwise—can enjoy.

1 large, ripe banana, mashed

⅓ cup mild vegetable oil

⅓ cup nondairy milk

1 (16-ounce) package Trader Joe's Gluten Free Brownie Baking Mix

½ cup semisweet chocolate chips, divided

½ (4.4-ounce) package Trader Joe's Nothing But...Banana, flattened

1 cup crushed Trader Joe's Banana Chips

VEGAN, GLUTEN-FREE

Preheat the oven to 350°F and lightly grease an 8-inch square baking pan or line the bottom with parchment paper. In a large bowl, mash the banana. Mix in the oil and milk with a whisk or spatula, and combine well. In 2 batches, add the brownie mix and stir until just combined. Spread half of the brownie-banana mixture into the prepared pan and sprinkle on ¼ cup of the chocolate chips. Peel out enough flattened banana slices to cover the first layer of the brownie mixture with 1 single layer. Spread the other half of the brownie-banana mixture over the banana layer. Sprinkle the top with the remaining ¼ cup chocolate chips and the banana chips. Bake until a toothpick inserted into the center comes out with moist crumbs, but no thick batter, 32 to 38 minutes. Let the brownies cool on a cooling rack for at least 25 minutes before serving.

MAKES: 16 brownies

I'M SO MAD ABOUT 'STACHIOS COOKIES

I love pistachios and I love chocolate and I love chewy, nummy oatmeal cookies. Isn't it great when everything just comes together? Trader Joe's is a fabulous place to get toasted, unsalted, and shelled pistachio nutmeats, perfect for a variety of treats! The pistachios add an intoxicating aromatic element to these cookies that makes eating them a multisensory experience. Deliciousness on all fronts!

½ cup ground Trader Joe's Dry Roasted & Unsalted Pistachio Nutmeats

¾ cup unbleached all-purpose flour

½ teaspoon baking powder

⅛ teaspoon sea salt

¾ cup Trader Joe's Organic Brown Sugar

1 egg

¼ cup mild vegetable oil

½ teaspoon vanilla extract

1 cup Trader Joe's Rolled Oats

⅓ cup chopped Trader Joe's Dry Roasted & Unsalted Pistachio Nutmeats

½ cup semisweet chocolate chips

Preheat the oven to 350°F and line a rimmed baking sheet with parchment paper. In a small bowl, combine the flour, ground pistachios, baking powder, and salt. In a large bowl, whisk together the brown sugar, egg, oil, and vanilla until well incorporated. Add the flour mixture in 2 batches. Add the oats in 2 batches, adding in the chopped pistachios and chocolate chips with the second batch. Mix well and let sit to allow the oats to absorb the moisture, about 10 minutes. Scoop out tablespoons of dough and lightly flatten, placing them about 1 inch apart on the baking sheet. Because of the nature of oatmeal cookies, they might crumble a bit on the edges when you do this, but just go ahead and gently shape them back together. Bake until the edges are set, but not browned, 8 to 9 minutes. Let the baking sheet cool on a cooling rack for 15 minutes, before transferring the cookies directly to the rack to finish cooling.

MAKES: 2 dozen cookies

. . . .

VEGAN OPTION: Replace the egg with ¼ cup unsweetened applesauce.

. . . .

HASTY PASTIES

These dessert pasties are super delicious and very quick to make. While I lean more toward pumpkin and apple butters, you can use any sort of jam or filling for these.

unbleached all-purpose flour, for dusting

1 sheet frozen Trader Joe's Pie Crusts, thawed according to package directions

optional fillings: Trader Joe's Honey Apple Butter, Pumpkin Butter, or Fig Butter

Preheat the oven to 375°F. Line a rimmed baking sheet with parchment paper for easy cleanup, or leave the sheet ungreased. Lightly dust a clean surface with flour and roll out the pie crust to ¼-inch thickness. Cut out the dough into 3-inch disks. Combine and roll out the scraps and make as many disks as you can, even in number. On top of half of the disks, scoop out about 1 tablespoon of the filling of your choice. Top with another disk and press the edges together to seal. If the dough isn't sticking well, lightly moisten it with water. Place the completed pasties on the prepared baking sheet. Cut a small hole on top of each pasty to vent. Bake until lightly browned, 12 to 15 minutes. Let cool on the baking sheet for 10 minutes before transferring to a cooling rack to cool completely.

MAKES: 5 to 7 pasties

VEGAN OPTION: Use 1 Vegan Pie Crust (recipe follows) in place of the TJ's crust.

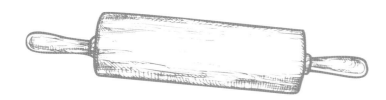

VEGAN PIE CRUST

This crust is very versatile and so tender and delicious…no one will think twice about whether its buttery goodness is vegan.

1¼ cups unbleached all-purpose flour

2 teaspoons Trader Joe's Organic Evaporated Cane Juice Sugar

⅛ teaspoon salt

½ cup cold Trader Joe's Vegan Buttery Spread, cut into chunks

2 to 4 tablespoons cold water

VEGAN

In a food processor or a medium bowl, combine the flour, sugar, and salt. If using the food processor, pulse or mix a few times to blend. Add the spread and pulse until the mixture becomes a coarse meal. If making by hand, cut in the spread using the back of a fork or a dough blender. Slowly add the water, 1 tablespoon at a time, until a dough comes together. Wrap the dough in plastic wrap and refrigerate for at least 1 hour before using. The dough can be frozen up to 1 month.

MAKES: Crust for 1 (9-inch) pie

QUICK KHEER

Kheer, a traditional Indian dessert, is a thin, spice-scented rice pudding sprinkled with raisins and cashews. It's delicious, and this version—with frozen rice—comes together incredibly quickly.

2 cups Trader Joe's frozen rice

1 cup Trader Joe's Light Coconut Milk (canned)

1 cup milk

3 tablespoons Trader Joe's Organic Evaporated Cane Juice Sugar

½ teaspoon ground cinnamon

¼ teaspoon vanilla extract

3 tablespoons Trader Joe's Raw Cashew Pieces

3 tablespoons Trader Joe's Golden Raisins

In a large saucepan over medium heat, combine the rice, coconut milk, and milk. Whisk to combine and bring to a simmer, being careful not to boil. Add the sugar and allow the mixture to simmer until much of the liquid has been absorbed into the rice but it is still soupy, about 15 minutes. Add the cinnamon, vanilla, cashews, and raisins, and cook for about 5 minutes more to allow the flavors to marry. Serve warm. Leftovers keep well in the fridge, but might need a little extra milk upon reheating.

MAKES: 4 servings

VEGAN OPTION: Replace the milk with a nondairy milk.

PAPPY'S PISTACHIO PUDDING

Pistachio pudding was something special I shared with my grandfather as a child and I can't think of it without getting the warm fuzzies. Ditch the boxed green stuff and whip up a batch of the real deal—you'll never go back. A coffee grinder or small food processor works best for grinding the pistachios as fine as you can get them.

½ cup Trader Joe's Organic Evaporated Cane Juice Sugar

2 tablespoons cornstarch

½ cup finely ground Trader Joe's Dry Roasted & Unsalted Pistachio Nutmeats

2 cups milk

¼ teaspoon vanilla extract

GLUTEN-FREE

In a large saucepan, whisk together the sugar and cornstarch until well blended. Whisk in the ground pistachios. Slowly whisk in the milk. Cook the pudding over medium high heat, whisking often, until it comes to a light boil. Whisking constantly, let lightly boil for about 2 minutes. Reduce the heat to low and continue to whisk constantly until the mixture thickens and coats the back of a spoon, 5 to 8 more minutes. If you're having problems with the pistachios clumping up a bit, you can always blend a little with an immersion blender. Remove from the heat and add the vanilla, mixing well. Transfer to 4 small heat-resistant bowls. Let cool completely before eating.

MAKES: 4 (½-cup) servings

VEGAN OPTION: Replace the milk with a nondairy milk; I recommend oat or hemp.

FALL PUMPKIN SPICE COBBLER

Oh boy. Pumpkin and spice and apples and pears—it doesn't get more fall than this. The cobbler topping is tender and fragrant while the apples and pears add delicious flavor and texture. On its own or à la mode, this dessert is the best. For optimal flavor, use a variety of apples and pears, particularly tart apples like Granny Smith or Pink Lady.

3 cups apples, peeled and sliced to ½-inch-thick slices (about 3 medium apples)

3 cups pears, peeled and sliced to ½-inch-thick slices (about 3 medium pears)

⅓ cup Trader Joe's Organic Evaporated Cane Juice Sugar

3 tablespoons cold unsalted butter

1 cup unbleached all-purpose flour

1½ teaspoons Trader Joe's Pumpkin Pie Spice

1 teaspoon ground cinnamon

1 teaspoon baking powder

⅛ teaspoon salt

1 cup Trader Joe's canned Organic Pumpkin

½ cup Trader Joe's Organic Brown Sugar

¼ cup mild vegetable oil

2 tablespoons milk

Preheat the oven to 350°F and lightly grease an 8-inch square baking pan. Layer the apples and pears on the bottom of the pan, packing them in tightly. They will shrink considerably while baking. While layering, divide and sprinkle the cane sugar on top of each layer. Cut up the cold butter into small pieces and sprinkle on top of the fruit. In a small bowl, combine the flour, pumpkin pie spice, cinnamon, baking powder, and salt. In a medium bowl, stir together the pumpkin, brown sugar, oil, and milk until well combined. Add the dry ingredients to the wet ingredients and mix until just incorporated. Spoon the batter over the top of the fruit layer. It may not cover the whole top, but don't worry because it will spread while baking. Bake until the pumpkin layer is lightly browned, there is bubbling juice around the edges, and a toothpick inserted into the center comes out clean, 45 to 50 minutes. Let the cobbler cool for at least 30 minutes before serving, so the sauce can thicken.

MAKES: 9 to 12 servings

VEGAN OPTION: Replace the butter and milk with nondairy equivalents.

GINGERED BREAD PUDDING

Bread pudding tends to divide people into two camps: the lovers and the haters. This particular bread pudding, with its moist composition studded with chocolate and ginger, is sure to break down the walls that divide.

4 to 5 cups torn French bread

3 eggs

½ cup Trader Joe's Organic Evaporated Cane Juice Sugar

2¼ cups milk

2 inches fresh ginger, peeled and finely grated

1 teaspoon vanilla extract

½ teaspoon ground cinnamon

½ cup semisweet chocolate chips

½ cup chopped Trader Joe's Candied Ginger

Preheat the oven to 375°F and lightly grease a 9 x 5-inch loaf pan. Place the torn bread into a large bowl. In a medium bowl, whisk together the eggs and sugar until the yolks are broken and the mixture is creamy. Add the milk, fresh ginger, vanilla, and cinnamon, and whisk until combined. Pour the egg mixture over the bread and mix well to combine. You want the bread to be soaked through with the liquids. Add the chocolate chips and candied ginger and gently incorporate. Spread the bread mixture into the prepared pan, pouring any leftover egg mixture from the bowl over the top. Bake until a knife inserted into the center of the loaf comes out clean, 55 to 60 minutes. Let cool on a cooling rack for at least 30 minutes before serving.

MAKES: 10 to 12 slices

VEGAN OPTION: Replace the eggs with ½ cup of pureed tofu and replace the milk with a nondairy substitute, increasing the amount to 2⅓ cups.

AMAZING EVERYTHING COOKIES

These cookies incorporate everything that is good and holy in the world: peanut butter, bananas, walnuts, and chocolate. Together, they create a super cookie that's sure to bring peace to the mouths of all who eat it. No joke.

1 cup unbleached all-purpose flour

1 teaspoon baking soda

¼ teaspoon salt

½ cup unsalted butter, at room temperature

¾ cup Trader Joe's Organic Evaporated Cane Juice Sugar

½ cup Trader Joe's Valencia Peanut Butter

¼ cup milk

½ teaspoon vanilla extract

⅓ cup semisweet chocolate chips or chopped Trader Joe's Pound Plus chocolate bar

⅓ cup Trader Joe's California Walnut Baking Pieces

⅓ cup crushed Trader Joe's Banana Chips

Preheat the oven to 350°F and line 2 rimmed baking sheets with parchment paper. In a small bowl, combine the flour, baking soda, and salt. In a large bowl, cream together the butter and sugar until smooth. Add the peanut butter and incorporate well. Add the milk and vanilla and mix thoroughly. In 2 batches, add the dry ingredients to the wet ingredients. Then add the chocolate chips or chocolate bar pieces, walnuts, and banana chips, and mix until just incorporated. Scoop out tablespoons of the dough and place 2 inches apart on the prepared baking sheets. Bake until the cookies are golden and the edges are set, 9 to 11 minutes. Remove from the oven and let cool for 10 minutes before transferring to a cooling rack to cool completely.

MAKES: 2 dozen cookies

VEGAN OPTION: Replace the butter and milk with nondairy equivalents.

BEST CHEESECAKE

When you put the word "best" in the title of a recipe, you better be ready to deliver. This cheesecake is unbelievable; it's creamy, melt-in-your-mouth velvety and not too sweet, and has just enough crust. It definitely deserves the title. It's perfect as is, but it's still fun to dress it up with fresh fruit, or try the simple variation below.

CRUST:

1 cup crushed Trader Joe's Honey Graham Crackers

3 tablespoons melted unsalted butter

1 tablespoon Trader Joe's Organic Evaporated Cane Juice Sugar

CAKE:

16 ounces cream cheese

1 cup sour cream

1 cup Trader Joe's Organic Evaporated Cane Juice Sugar

2 teaspoons vanilla extract

4 eggs, separated

Preheat the oven to 350°F.

To make the crust: Combine the graham cracker crumbs, butter, and sugar in a bowl and mix well, until it has the consistency of sand. Press the crumb mixture into the bottom and up the walls of an ungreased 8- or 9-inch springform pan.

To make the cake: In the bowl of a food processor or blender, process the cream cheese, sour cream, sugar, vanilla, and the egg yolks to combine. In a second medium bowl, using a handheld mixer, whip the egg whites until they make stiff peaks. Gently pulse to add the egg whites to the cheesecake mixture. Pour the batter over the crust. Bake until the top of the cake is lightly browned and the edges are set (the center will still be a little jiggly), 50 to 60 minutes, depending on the size of the pan. Let the cake cool on a wire rack, then cover and chill completely in the fridge for at least 4 hours, preferably overnight, before serving.

MAKES: 8 to 10 slices

VEGAN OPTION: See the Best Vegan Cheesecake (recipe follows).

GLUTEN-FREE OPTION: TJ's makes gluten-free gingersnaps—swap them out for the graham crackers and you have a gluten-free crust!

BEST VEGAN CHEESECAKE

Vegan cheesecakes are often characterized as being thick and dense, but this cake has a creamy texture that will please vegans and nonvegans alike. You can forgo making the graham cracker crust and use a premade one, as many of them are vegan. Be sure to plan ahead, as this needs to cool completely and then chill in the fridge for several hours before serving. You can use a flavored yogurt in place of the soy if you have it handy, because you won't taste the flavor in the finished cheesecake.

CRUST:

1½ cups crushed vegan graham crackers

4 tablespoons Trader Joe's Vegan Buttery Spread

1 tablespoon Trader Joe's Organic Evaporated Cane Juice Sugar

CAKE:

1 (8-ounce) container Trader Joe's Vegan Cream Cheese Alternative

¾ cup Trader Joe's creamy cultured cashew yogurt

1½ cups medium tofu, drained and pureed

1 cup Trader Joe's Organic Evaporated Cane Juice Sugar

2 teaspoons vanilla extract

1 teaspoon lemon juice

VEGAN

Preheat the oven to 350°F.

To make the crust: In a small bowl, combine the graham cracker crumbs, spread, and sugar, and mix well, until it has the consistency of sand. Press into the bottom and up the sides of an ungreased 9-inch pie pan.

To make the cake: In the bowl of a food processor or in a blender, process the cream cheese alternative, yogurt, tofu, sugar, vanilla, and lemon juice, scraping down the sides as needed, until incorporated. Pour the cheesecake filling into the crust. Bake until the edges are set and the cake is light golden brown, 50 to 60 minutes. The center will be slightly jiggly. Let the cake cool completely on a cooling rack, about 2 hours, before transferring to the fridge. Chill for at least 4 hours, or preferably overnight, before serving. Serve with fruit or another topping of your choice.

MAKES: 8 to 10 slices

CHEWY MOCHA ICE CREAM CAKE

Wow. This ice cream cake features a bottom brownie layer that's topped with a generous layer of ice cream and finished off with a soft ganache topping. It's chewy, creamy, and intensely chocolatey. Basically, it's perfect. Patience is a virtue, as the brownie layer needs to cool before the finished cake can set in the freezer.

CAKE BATTER:

½ cup milk

¼ teaspoon mild vinegar

¼ cup mild vegetable oil

1 (16-ounce) box Trader Joe's Brownie Truffle Baking Mix

1 (32-ounce) container of Coffee Bean Blast ice cream

GANACHE:

¼ cup semisweet chocolate chips

1 tablespoon milk

2 tablespoons Trader Joe's Vegan Buttery Spread

VEGAN

Preheat the oven to 350°F and lightly grease the bottom only of an 8- or 9-inch springform pan. In a large bowl, whisk together the milk and vinegar and let sit for several minutes. Stir in the vegetable oil. In 2 batches, incorporate the brownie mix until just combined. Spread in the bottom of the prepared pan and bake until a toothpick comes out with a few moist crumbs, but no batter, 25 to 32 minutes, depending on the size of the pan. Let the brownies cool completely in the pan on a cooling rack. While the brownies are cooling, take the ice cream out of the freezer and let it thaw until it's smooth and spreadable, but still solid. Once the brownies are cool, spread the ice cream smoothly on top of them. Freeze for 1 hour to set before topping with the ganache.

To make the ganache: In a microwave-safe bowl, melt the chocolate chips and milk in 15- to 20-second increments, stirring between each interval. Once the chocolate is melted, whisk well to incorporate into the milk. Add the spread and mix well. Drizzle the ganache in lines across the top of the firm ice cream cake. Return the cake to the freezer for at least 2 more hours. Run a knife around the outside of the pan to loosen the brownie bottom before releasing the sides of the pan, then serve.

MAKES: 10 to 12 servings

VEGAN OPTION: There are loads of vegan ice cream options at TJ's. Try their Oat milk Strawberry for a refreshing, and dairy-free twist.

HOMEMADE DULCE DE LECHE

Okay, really? A one-ingredient recipe? Consider this more of a technique—a master class in kitchen alchemy. Sweetened condensed milk, heat, and time are all you need for a can of the richest, sweetest dulce de leche you've ever tasted. I always make several cans at a time, you never know when you'll want to pop one open to dip fruit into, drizzle over ice cream, or just eat with a spoon.

1 (10-ounce) can Trader Joe's Organic Sweetened Condensed Milk

GLUTEN-FREE

STOVETOP METHOD:

Remove the paper label from the unopened can. Fill a pot with water so the can is submerged at least 1 inch over the top. Bring the water to a boil, then cover the pot with a lid and reduce the heat to bring the water to a simmer. Cook for 2 to 3 hours (depending on how dark you want your dulce), making sure at least 1 inch of water remains above the can. When done, remove from the heat but let the can cool in the water before removing to continue cooling on a hot pad. Do not open the can until it is fully cooled.

PRESSURE-COOKER METHOD:

Place a kitchen towel in the bottom of the pressure cooker. Remove the paper label from the unopened can. Place the can on top of the towel and submerge in the water, at least 2 inches above the top of the can, but not above the maximum fill line. Attach the lid and cook at high pressure for 15 minutes. Allow the pressure to come down naturally (do NOT release). Once the pressure is gone, remove the lid and allow the can to cool to room temperature. Do not open the can until it is fully cooled.

MAKES: 1 heaping cup

CASHEW NIBBLE COOKIES

Eating these cookies is like eating warm, gooey bites of raw cookie dough. And you can feel relieved that they are full of real, healthy ingredients. What are you waiting for? Get baking!

1 cup Trader Joe's Raw Whole Cashews

5 Trader Joe's Fancy Medjool Dates

1 cup unbleached all-purpose flour

2 tablespoons Trader Joe's Organic Evaporated Cane Juice Sugar

½ teaspoon baking powder

⅛ teaspoon salt

2 tablespoons mild oil

2 tablespoons honey or Trader Joe's Organic Blue Agave Sweetener

¼ teaspoon vanilla extract

¼ to ⅓ cup chopped semisweet chocolate chips

In a small bowl, pour warm water over the cashews and let sit for about 1 hour. In a second small bowl, do the same with the dates. In a third small bowl, combine the flour, sugar, baking powder, and salt. Preheat the oven to 325°F and line a rimmed baking sheet with parchment paper. Drain the cashews and place in the bowl of a food processor. Process until mealy, 1 to 2 minutes. Drain the dates and add to the cashews, then process to a paste. There might be flecks of date skin, but that's okay. Add the oil, honey or agave, and vanilla, and pulse until incorporated. Add the flour mixture in 2 batches, until a soft dough comes together. Scoop out into a large bowl and fold in the chopped chocolate chips.

Using a small cookie scoop or a teaspoon, scoop out rounded bits of dough and place them ½ to ¾ inches apart on the prepared baking sheet; the cookies don't expand very much. Press down on the tops of the cookies with the back of a spoon to make them flat on top. Bake until they look a little golden and feel set on the edges, about 8 minutes. Remove the baking sheet from the oven and let cool for 5 minutes before transferring the cookies to a cooling rack. Store leftover cookies in a loosely covered container at room temperature.

MAKES: 50 niblets

VEGAN OPTION: Use the agave syrup rather than honey.

BACK-IN-THE-DAY DATE BARS

Betty Crocker would approve of this old-school revival. These date bars are delicious and very rich—a little goes a long way, which is great because it means you might actually be able to get them out of your kitchen to share with the rest of the world. Trader Joe's has such great prices on dates, and you'll surely add these bars to your regular rotation. Be sure to be patient and let the date mixture cool after cooking it; good things come to those who wait.

2 cups chopped pitted dates

½ cup water

¼ cup Trader Joe's Organic Maple Agave Syrup Blend

½ teaspoon vanilla extract

1 cup unbleached all-purpose flour

1 cup Trader Joe's Rolled Oats

½ teaspoon baking powder

½ teaspoon ground cinnamon

¼ teaspoon salt

⅓ cup Trader Joe's Organic Evaporated Cane Juice Sugar

⅓ cup mild vegetable oil

¼ cup milk

½ cup Trader Joe's Walnut Halves & Pieces

In a small saucepan, combine the dates, water, and maple-agave syrup. Bring to a simmer over medium heat and gently mash the dates. Cook until a thick paste comes together, about 10 minutes, stirring often. Remove from the heat, stir in the vanilla, then transfer the date mixture to a heatproof bowl and let cool completely. Preheat the oven to 400°F and lightly grease and flour an 8-inch square baking pan. In a small bowl, combine the flour, oats, baking powder, cinnamon, and salt. In a large bowl, cream together the sugar and oil. Add the milk and stir to combine. Add the dry ingredients to the wet ingredients in 2 batches, until just combined. Press 2 cups of the dough into the bottom of the prepared pan. Spread the cooled date mixture over the layer of dough. Add the walnuts to the remaining dough and crumble over the top of the date mixture. Gently press down the topping. Bake until the top is golden and the bars feel set, 20 to 25 minutes. Let cool completely on a cooling rack before slicing and serving.

MAKES: 16 to 20 bars

VEGAN OPTION: Replace the milk with a nondairy substitute.

APPLE UPSIDE-DOWN CAKE

This moist and tender cake can easily pair with coffee in the morning and be dressed up with a scoop of ice cream in the evening. It's the "little black dress" of cakes. Granny Smith and Pink Lady apples are both excellent choices.

1 tablespoon unsalted butter

¼ cup Trader Joe's Organic Brown Sugar

½ teaspoon fresh lemon juice

3 to 4 tart apples, peeled and sliced ½-inch-thick (about 4 cups)

1½ cups unbleached all-purpose flour

1½ teaspoons baking powder

1 teaspoon ground cinnamon

½ teaspoon salt

⅓ cup mild vegetable oil

¾ cup Trader Joe's Organic Evaporated Cane Juice Sugar

¼ cup unsweetened applesauce

¾ cup milk

1 teaspoon vanilla extract

Preheat the oven to 350°F. Lightly grease and flour an 8-inch round cake pan and line the bottom with parchment paper. Because this cake is inverted, it works best with parchment on the bottom, to ensure a clean release. In a large sauté pan or skillet, melt the butter over medium heat. Add the brown sugar and lemon juice, then add the apples and stir. Simmer until the apples are coated with the sugar mixture and slightly softened, about 10 minutes. Remove from the heat and let cool slightly. In a small bowl, combine the flour, baking powder, cinnamon, and salt. In a large bowl, cream together the oil and sugar. Add the applesauce, milk, and vanilla. In 2 batches, incorporate the dry mixture into the wet mixture.

Arrange the apple slices in the bottom of the prepared pan and drizzle any additional juices from the pan over the apples. Spread the cake batter over the top of the apples. Bake until a toothpick inserted into the center comes out clean, but with a couple of moist crumbs on it, 50 to 55 minutes. Remove the pan from the oven and let cool on a rack for 10 minutes. Run a knife along the edge of the pan and carefully invert the cake onto a serving dish. Let the cake sit for a minute or 2 before carefully lifting the pan off. Peel the parchment paper off of the cake and let it continue cooling for at least 20 minutes before serving.

MAKES: 10 to 12 slices of cake

VEGAN OPTION: Replace the butter with Trader Joe's Vegan Buttery Spread and the milk with nondairy milk.

FRUITY BROWN, BUTTERED CRISPY TREATS

Freeze-dried fruit is a baking revelation—intense fruit flavor without any of the unwanted moisture. The combination of tart apples, nutty browned butter, and a sprinkling of salt makes these crispy rice treats like a gooey spin on apple pie.

1 cup Trader Joe's Freeze Dried Fuji Apple Slices

½ cup (1 stick) plus 1 tablespoon unsalted butter, divided

1 (10-ounce) bag Trader Joe's Marshmallows (large or mini are fine)

¼ teaspoon sea salt

½ teaspoon ground cinnamon

5½ cups Trader Joe's Crispy Rice Cereal

GLUTEN-FREE

Butter and line an 8 x 8-inch pan with parchment paper and set aside. Finely crush the freeze-dried apples, either in a small food processor or in a ziplock bag (pound and roll the apples with a rolling pin). Some bigger chunks are okay, but you want the apples as pulverized as possible. Reserve 2 tablespoons and set both quantities aside.

In the bottom of a large pot, melt the ½ cup of butter over medium heat, stirring often, until it begins to froth and foam. It will be hard to see beneath the foam, but you'll hear the butter spitting and popping. At this point, stir continuously and the second it goes quiet, immediately remove from the heat. Add the tablespoon of butter and mix until melted. Immediately add the marshmallows and mix quickly to combine, allowing the heat to melt the marshmallows. Vegan marshmallows, if using, take a bit more work to melt, but a little elbow grease will do it. Once smooth, quickly add the bulk of the freeze-dried apples, salt, and cinnamon, and whisk to incorporate before adding the rice cereal. Once the cereal is well coated, spread it quickly in the prepared pan and top with the remaining apple dust. Allow to cool slightly before cutting.

MAKES: 1 dozen treats

PARSNIP CAKE WITH BROWNED BUTTER CREAM CHEESE FROSTING

Parsnips in cake aren't as crazy as they might seem. They are commonly incorporated into baking in the United Kingdom, and for good reason. A deep and earthy alternative to carrots, this cake is all grown up, enhanced by fragrant nutmeg.

1½ cups all-purpose flour

¾ cup Trader Joe's Organic Evaporated Cane Juice Sugar

2 teaspoons baking powder

1 tablespoon ground ginger

1½ teaspoons Trader Joe's Organic Ground Cinnamon

½ teaspoon ground nutmeg

¾ teaspoon salt

2 eggs

½ cup canola oil

½ cup milk

1 teaspoon vanilla extract

2 cups parsnips, peeled and finely shredded

1 recipe Browned Butter Cream Cheese Frosting (recipe below)

Preheat the oven to 350°F. Grease an 8 x 8-inch or 9 x 9-inch pan and line bottom with parchment paper. In a medium bowl, combine the flour, sugar, baking powder, ground ginger, cinnamon, nutmeg, and salt. In a large bowl, whisk together the eggs, canola oil, milk, and vanilla. Add the dry ingredients in 2 batches and stir until just mixed well. Gently mix in the parsnips.

Pour the batter into the prepared pan and bake for 25 to 30 minutes, until golden brown and a toothpick inserted in the center of the cake comes out clean. Cool completely on a rack before frosting with the Browned Butter Cream Cheese Frosting.

MAKES: 12 servings of cake

VEGAN OPTION: Replace the eggs with Trader Joe's Simply Eggless and the milk with a nondairy alternative.

COOK'S NOTE: If you're planning to use the Browned Butter Cream Cheese Frosting, brown the butter for that before you do anything else. The butter needs to cool enough to become soft but solid again, which takes some time (this process can be sped up by cooling it in the fridge or freezer.

BROWNED BUTTER CREAM CHEESE FROSTING

Sorry not sorry for introducing you to the reality-altering magic that happens when browned butter and cream cheese frosting come together. You'll never be able to accept classic cream cheese frosting again.

2 ounces (half a stick) unsalted butter

8 ounces cream cheese, at room temperature

¾ to 1¼ cups Trader Joe's Organic Powdered Sugar, sifted

½ teaspoon Trader Joe's Organic Vanilla Bean Paste

In a small saucepan, heat the butter over medium heat, stirring often, until it begins to froth and foam. It will be hard to see beneath the foam, but you'll hear the butter spitting and popping. At this point, stir continuously and the second it goes quiet, remove from the heat. Pour the butter into a small heat-safe bowl, getting any brown bits remaining. Allow to cool until solid again. You can speed this up in the fridge or freezer. Browned butter will be slightly softer than regular, taking on a spreadable consistency, even once it's firmed up.

In the bottom of a large bowl, whip the solid browned butter until it's soft then add the cream cheese, mixing until creamy. Add the powdered sugar (starting small) along with the vanilla. Combine to desired sweetness. If the frosting gets too thick, you can add a splash of milk to smooth it out. If you can resist eating it all with a spoon, swirl the frosting over the Parsnip Cake (page 186) or, honestly, anything you can get your hands on.

MAKES: enough for one 9 x 9- inch cake

EASY FRUIT AND CHEESECAKE GALETTE

This simple galette is the perfect foil to showcase any seasonal fruit but truly shines with summer stone fruit. Peaches, apricot, plums...the list goes on and on.

GALETTE:

1 Trader Joe's Pie Crusts (½ a box)

⅓ to ½ cup Trader Joe's Organic Evaporated Cane Juice Sugar (less if the fruit is very ripe)

1 teaspoon cornstarch

sprinkle of salt

3 to 4 cups sliced fruit (depending on how tall you want the galette to be), sliced ½ inch thick

CHEESECAKE CREAM:

8 ounces cream cheese, at room temperature

⅓ cup Trader Joe's Organic Evaporated Cane Juice Sugar

1 egg, separated

2 teaspoons lemon juice

1 teaspoon vanilla

splash of milk

raw sugar, for sprinkling

On a baking sheet covered with a large piece of parchment paper, roll out the pie crust to roughly a 14-inch circle. Place it in fridge until ready to use. In a large bowl, combine the sugar, cornstarch, and salt, and whisk together to break up any clumps. Add the sliced fruit and toss to combine. Set aside. For the cheesecake cream, in a medium bowl, cream the cream cheese, using a hand mixer, until smooth. Add the sugar, egg yolk, lemon juice, and vanilla, and mix until well combined. Retrieve the chilled crust from the fridge. Spread half of the cream cheese mixture over the bottom of the crust, stopping 2 to 3 inches from the edge. Pile the fruit on top the cream cheese circle, scraping out any residual sugar/juices from the bowl (I usually do this over the middle of the fruit mound). Arrange the fruit into a mostly level mound, slightly higher in the middle, then fold the edge of the crust up and over the fruit—some parts of the crust will overlap, so feel free to pinch them together if it helps the crust stay put. Gently smooth the remaining cream cheese filling over the top of the fruit, leaving a perimeter of fruit exposed.

In a small bowl, whisk together the egg white and a splash of milk. Brush the egg wash over the edge of the crust and sprinkle with raw sugar.

Return the galette to the fridge to chill while preheating the oven to 350°F, about 10 to 15 minutes. Bake for 40 to 50 minutes, until the crust is golden brown and the filling looks set. The fruit should look juicy. Let cool for at least 30 minutes before serving.

MAKES: 6 large slices

LEMON GINGER ICE BOX CAKE

The combination of lemon and ginger is classic for a reason, but the addition of richly spiced Speculoos cookies, tangy crème fraîche, and spicy candied ginger make this simple, make- ahead "cake" an elegant option for dessert, any time of year.

1 (7.5-ounce) container Trader Joe's Crème Fraîche, at room temperature

½ cup Trader Joe's Powdered Sugar

zest of 1 lemon

2½ cups Trader Joe's Heavy Whipping Cream

½ teaspoon Trader Joe's Ground Ginger

½ teaspoon vanilla extract

2 (7-ounce) sleeves of Trader Joe's Speculoos Cookies

1 cup Trader Joe's Imported English Authentic Lemon Curd

½ cup Trader Joe's Crystallized Candied Ginger, chopped

Line a 9 x 5-inch loaf pan with plastic wrap, all the way up all 4 sides with overhang over the sides. In the bowl of a stand mixer or in a large bowl with a hand mixer, whip the crème fraîche, powdered sugar, and lemon zest on medium speed until smooth. Add the heavy cream, ground ginger, and vanilla, and continue to mix on medium speed until medium peaks form, about 3 minutes.

Spread a thin layer of the crème fraîche mixture on the bottom of the pan, then cover it with a single layer of Speculoos cookies. Top the cookies with about 2 tablespoons of the lemon curd then one-quarter of the crème fraîche mixture, using a spatula or the back of a spoon to even it out. Repeat the layers, finishing with the last layer of crème fraîche. Cover the pan with plastic wrap and freeze for 3 hours. To serve, unmold the cake over a platter and carefully remove the plastic wrap. Top with candied ginger and slice while still frozen.

MAKES: 12 servings

TAHINI-DOODLES

Nutty tahini and cardamom take the classic snickerdoodle to a whole new level, making it the first cookie you reach for rather than the last.

COATING:

⅓ cup granulated sugar

1 teaspoon Trader Joe's Organic Ground Cinnamon

½ teaspoon ground cardamom

COOKIES:

2¾ cups all-purpose flour

2 teaspoons cream of tartar

1 teaspoon baking soda

1 teaspoon Trader Joe's Organic Ground Cinnamon

½ teaspoon ground cardamom

½ teaspoon sea salt

1 cup (2 sticks) unsalted butter, at room temperature

1⅓ cup (267 grams) granulated sugar

¼ cup Trader Joe's Organic Tahini

1 large egg plus 1 egg yolk

2 teaspoons vanilla bean paste

Preheat the oven to 375°F. Line a large baking sheet with parchment paper. For the coating, in a small bowl, combine the sugar, cinnamon, and cardamom together in a small bowl.

For the cookies, in a medium bowl, whisk the flour, cream of tartar, baking soda, cinnamon, cardamom, and salt. In the bowl of a stand mixer or using a large bowl and a hand mixer, beat the butter and sugar together until smooth and creamy, about 2 minutes. Add the tahini, egg, egg yolk, and vanilla extract until well combined. Add the dry ingredients in 3 batches until just combined.

Scoop the cookie dough into balls, about 2 tablespoons in size. Roll the dough balls in the coating. Set the cookies 3 inches apart on the prepared baking sheets. Bake the cookies for 9 to 10 minutes. They will be puffy but have some slight cracks. While cooling, they will collapse a bit. Let cool on the baking sheet for 5 minutes before transferring to a cooling rack.

MAKES: 2½ dozen cookies

FIG DELIGHT

This dessert is tender, sweet, and complex. It's the perfect light ending to a heavier meal or as a treat on a hot summer day.

¼ cup red wine or grape juice

12 Trader Joe's Black Mission Figs

8 (¼-inch) slices from a log of sweet chèvre, such as Trader Joe's Chèvre With Honey Goat's Milk Cheese

¼ cup honey

In a small saucepan over medium low heat, simmer the wine or grape juice with the figs until tender and plump, about 10 minutes. Remove from the heat and let cool. Place 2 slices of cheese on each of 4 plates. Top with 3 figs and 2 tablespoons honey each.

MAKES: 4 servings

VEGAN OPTION: Omit the cheese. In its place, combine 6 ounces Trader Joe's Vegan Cream Cheese Alternative with 1 teaspoon lemon juice and 2 teaspoons Trader Joe's Organic Maple Agave Syrup Blend. Divide that mixture among the plates and serve as directed, substituting more maple-agave or regular agave syrup for the honey.

SCOUT'S HONOR MACAROONS

Imagine the classic Girl Scout cookie, but fresh and rich, filled with the very best dulce de leche, coconut, and the contrast of semisweet chocolate.

2 cups Trader Joe's Organic Unsweetened Flake Coconut

⅔ cup Homemade Dulce de Leche (page 181)

1 teaspoon vanilla extract

2 large egg whites

⅛ teaspoon salt

1 tablespoon Trader Joe's Organic Evaporated Cane Juice Sugar

1 cup Trader Joe's Semi-Sweet Chocolate Chunks

GLUTEN-FREE

In a large bowl, combine the coconut, dulce de leche, and vanilla. Mix to coat and set aside. In a separate medium bowl, whip the egg whites and salt until soft peaks form. Add the sugar and whip until glossy, about 30 seconds. In 2 batches, add the sugared egg whites to the coconut mixture and fold to combine. The eggs will deflate, but don't worry about it. Let the mixture sit at room temperature for 20 to 30 minutes to let the coconut hydrate. While waiting, preheat the oven to 350°F.

Line a baking sheet with parchment paper and scoop the macaroons onto the sheet with a large cookie or ice cream scoop (about ¼ cup), 2 inches apart. Bake for 15 to 18 minutes, until golden brown. Because of the dulce de leche, they will look a little darker than the average macaroon. Let cool completely on a cooling rack. Melt the chocolate in the microwave in short, 15-second intervals or over a double boiler. Dip the bottoms of the macaroons in the melted chocolate and place back on the parchment-lined baking sheets to set. Scrape the remaining chocolate into a small ziplock baggie. Snip a bottom corner off of the baggie and drizzle the chocolate over the tops of the macaroons.

MAKES: 18 cookies

Beverages

Sometimes you need a liquid lunch. Not *that* kind of liquid lunch, but a hot-day-cold-smoothie kind of lunch. Or a rich-and-thick-mocha-milkshake kind of dessert. Or a bubbly fruity-spritzer kind of refreshment. Or a warm-creamy-spicy-cuppa with cookies. No matter what time of day or year, turn to these drinks to fulfill your needs.

- MOCHA MILKSHAKE
- BERRNANA NO-MILKSHAKE
- GREAT GREEN SMOOTHIE
- GRAPE LIME SLUSH
- TASTY CUBES
- RASPBERRY TEA SYRUP
- GINGER SPARKLING ALE
- MANGO LASSI
- CREAMY COCONUT CHAI
- SPECTOOCULAR HOT CHOCOLATE
- FESTIVE PUNCH

MOCHA MILKSHAKE

Coffee and chocolate and milkshakes…I can't imagine anything better! This treat is fast to make and goes down nice and easy on a hot day.

¼ cup milk

2 teaspoons Trader Joe's 100% Colombian Instant Coffee

3 tablespoons Trader Joe's Organic Midnight Moo Chocolate Flavored Syrup

4 to 5 large scoops vanilla ice cream

In a small cup, whisk together the milk and the instant coffee. You might need to slightly heat the milk in the microwave for just a few seconds on high heat to help the coffee dissolve. If so, let it cool before using. In a blender, combine the coffee mixture, chocolate syrup, and ice cream, and blend until smooth and incorporated.

MAKES: 2 milkshakes

VEGAN OPTION: Replace the ice cream and milk with nondairy options and use a nondairy chocolate syrup.

BERRNANA NO-MILKSHAKE

Frozen, creamy bananas take the place of ice cream in this fruity milkshake.

2 large, ripe frozen bananas

1½ cups Trader Joe's Very Cherry Berry Blend (in the frozen section)

¾ to 1¼ cups milk

1 to 2 tablespoons Trader Joe's Organic Maple Agave Syrup Blend (optional)

GLUTEN-FREE

Combine the bananas, cherry blend, milk, and maple-agave syrup, if using, in a blender and blend until smooth, adding enough milk and maple-agave syrup, if using, to reach the desired consistency and sweetness.

MAKES: 2 shakes

VEGAN OPTION: Use a nondairy milk such as soy or hemp to get the creamiest shake.

GREAT GREEN SMOOTHIE

If adding greens to a smoothie sounds scary, suspend your disbelief for a moment and take this recipe for a whirl. The result is sweet and smooth, and it will take only one sip to make you a believer.

1 cup Trader Joe's Kale

½ cup Trader Joe's Organics Baby Spinach

½ cup Trader Joe's Pineapple Tidbits (in the frozen section)

½ cup Trader Joe's Mango Chunks (in the frozen section)

1 large frozen ripe banana, in chunks

½ to 1 cup orange juice

2 teaspoons Trader Joe's Coconut Oil

2 to 3 ice cubes

VEGAN, GLUTEN-FREE

Combine all the ingredients in a blender. Process until smooth, adjusting the orange juice if necessary to reach the desired consistency. You may need to scrape down and adjust the contents of the blender base to thoroughly process the greens.

MAKES: 2 smoothies

GRAPE LIME SLUSH

This slushy is a little sweet, a little tart, and a little bubbly—perfect!

2 cups red grapes

1 very thinly sliced peeled lime

½ cup ice

1 cup Trader Joe's Lime Sparkling Spring Water

VEGAN, GLUTEN-FREE

In a food processor or blender, combine the grapes, lime, and ice. Blend until thick and well-combined. Divide into 2 glasses and top each with ½ cup of the sparkling water.

MAKES: 2 servings

TASTY CUBES

Someone in my family (who, for their own protection, will remain nameless) recently admitted to me that they don't like the taste of water. Water. While I don't particularly understand this concept myself, I can totally appreciate a jazzed-up glass of H_2O. A great way to have lots of flavor options at the drop of a hat is to have fancy ice cubes. Here are some suggested cubes, but let your imagination run wild.

CUKE CUBES:

Add freshly washed, peeled cucumber chunks to an ice cube tray and cover with water. For an extra dose of refreshment, add a sprig of mint as well.

CREAMY CUBES:

Trader Joe's Light Coconut Milk (canned) makes a delicious tray of great cubes, not only to infuse a glass of water, but also to dunk in a cup of iced coffee.

TANGY BERRY CUBES:

Muddle fresh or frozen berries with a hint of liquid sweetener, such as Trader Joe's Organic Maple Agave Syrup Blend, and fresh lemon juice. Top off with water.

ZESTY CUBES:

Rather than tossing the rinds from your oranges, freeze chunks of them in water to perk up your drink on a hot day.

RASPBERRY TEA SYRUP

This thick, sweet raspberry syrup takes iced tea from refreshing to redonkulous. It's also quite tasty over ice cream.

2⅓ cups frozen Trader Joe's Frozen Raspberries

¼ cup Trader Joe's Organic Maple Agave Syrup Blend

8 ounces Trader Joe's Kettle Brewed Unsweetened Black iced tea

VEGAN, GLUTEN-FREE

In a small saucepan, combine the berries and maple-agave syrup. Over medium low heat, stir often until the berries soften and form a syrup, about 5 minutes. Crush the berries with the back of a spoon. Bring to a simmer and cook until reduced and the sauce coats the back of a spoon, about 10 minutes. Strain the mixture through a fine-mesh sieve to remove most of the seeds. Store the syrup in a small bottle, refrigerated, for up to 2 weeks. To make a raspberry iced tea, combine 1 to 2 tablespoons of the syrup with the iced tea, adjusting to your preference.

MAKES: ½ cup of syrup

GINGER SPARKLING ALE

Not only does my homemade ginger syrup make a mean ginger ale, it also tastes great over ice cream or with yogurt! You could also use it in a cocktail, if you were so inclined. Ginger love for all!

1¼ cups water

⅓ cup Trader Joe's Organic Evaporated Cane Juice Sugar

3 to 4 tablespoons freshly grated ginger

¼ teaspoon vanilla extract

8 ounces Trader Joe's Sparkling Spring Water

VEGAN, GLUTEN-FREE

In a medium saucepan over medium high heat, combine the water and sugar. Bring to a boil, stirring often, then lower the heat to a simmer. Add the ginger, starting with less and increasing the amount based on your tolerance and preference, and cook until the sugar is dissolved, stirring constantly, about 5 minutes. Remove from the heat and then whisk in the vanilla. Let the syrup cool before using. Combine 1 to 2 tablespoons of syrup with the sparkling water. Gently whisk to combine. Store unused syrup in a sealed container at room temperature for up to 2 weeks.

MAKES: 1¼ cups of syrup

MANGO LASSI

Mango lassi is a traditional Indian drink, served to help quell the heat from spicy dishes and to showcase some tasty mango goodness. It's so simple, there's no excuse not to whip up a few the next time you bust out your curry powder!

¾ cup Trader Joe's Mango Chunks (in the frozen section), thawed

2½ cups plain or vanilla Trader Joe's Yogurt

1 tablespoon Trader Joe's Organic Maple Agave Syrup Blend or Trader Joe's Organic Blue Agave Sweetener (optional)

sea salt

GLUTEN-FREE

In a blender or food processor, combine the mango and yogurt. Blend until smooth. Taste and add sweetener as needed, if using. Divide the mixture into glasses and top with a light sprinkle of sea salt.

MAKES: 2 servings

VEGAN OPTION: Replace the yogurt with Trader Joe's Organic Vanilla Soy Yogurt.

COOK'S NOTE: I recommend using a low-fat or 1 percent yogurt in this, as it's thinner and makes for a better lassi consistency.

CREAMY COCONUT CHAI

This chai is rich and full of spice, a perfect indulgence on a cold day. Enjoy it with a tasty baked good, like Quinoa Breakfast Bread (page 24), and you have yourself one nice morning.

1 cup water

3 Trader Joe's Organic Ruby Red Chai tea bags

¼ teaspoon ground cinnamon

2 to 3 tablespoons Trader Joe's Organic Maple Agave Syrup Blend or Trader Joe's Organic Blue Agave Sweetener

½ cup milk

½ cup Trader Joe's Light Coconut Milk (canned)

GLUTEN-FREE

In a small saucepan, bring the water to a simmer over medium heat and then add the tea bags. Simmer for 5 minutes, then reduce the heat to low. Remove the bags, being sure to squeeze them out. Add the cinnamon and syrup, or agave sweetener and whisk well to combine. Remove from the heat and then add the milk and coconut milk, stirring until heated through. Divide into 2 cups, sprinkling the tops with additional cinnamon if desired.

MAKES: 2 servings

VEGAN OPTION: Replace the milk with a nondairy alternative.

COOK'S NOTE: Freeze leftover coconut milk in ice cube trays, then store in freezer bags. That way you have a couple of tablespoons of coconut milk when needed.

SPECTOOCULAR HOT CHOCOLATE

Trader Joe's has managed to once again outdo itself, this time by adding Speculoos Cookie Butter to its shelves. If you've never had it, do yourself a favor and pick up a jar. It's the equivalent of a spreadable nut butter except instead of being made from nuts, it's made from cookies. You heard me right—it's spreadable cookies!

3 tablespoons Trader Joe's Unsweetened Cocoa Powder

1 tablespoon plus 1 teaspoon Trader Joe's Organic Evaporated Cane Juice Sugar

2½ cups milk

2 tablespoons Trader Joe's Speculoos Cookie Butter

In a small saucepan, whisk together the cocoa and sugar. Slowly whisk in the milk, and heat until it comes to a simmer, whisking constantly. Whisk in the cookie butter and gently whisk until melted and incorporated. Divide into 2 mugs.

MAKES: 2 servings

VEGAN OPTION: Replace the milk with a nondairy option. Lucky you, Speculoos is vegan!

FESTIVE PUNCH

This recipe results in a large amount of punch, but it can easily be scaled down for smaller servings. If the kiddos won't be around, you can also spike this brew with rum for the grown-ups. Yum! I make this in a stockpot on the stove, to keep it warm.

1 (12-ounce) bag fresh Trader Joe's Cranberries

¼ cup Trader Joe's Organic Evaporated Cane Juice Sugar

1 (64-ounce) bottle Trader Joe's Spiced Cider

2 (3-inch) slices of orange rind

VEGAN, GLUTEN-FREE

In a stockpot, combine the cranberries and sugar. Cook over medium low heat until the cranberries begin to soften and their juices run, about 10 minutes. Muddle them with a potato masher to combine with the sugar. Add the cider, increase the heat to medium high and bring to a gentle boil for about 5 minutes. Lower to a simmer and add the orange rind. Simmer, covered, for at least 10 minutes.

MAKES: 8 to 10 servings

Sample Menus

Menu planning is one of my all-time favorite things to do. Poring over recipes and flavor profiles and dreaming up the perfect pairings to wow my guests…it's addictive. But sometimes you don't want to work that hard or don't have the time. That's where these quick menus come into play.

FANCY BRUNCH

Tasty Tofu Scramble (page 23)

Banana Cinnamon Rolls (page 13) and Peanut Butter Cream Cheese Frosting (page 14)

Simple Fruit Salad (page 70)

HANGOVER BRUNCH

The Ultimate Waffle (page 34)

Great Green Smoothie (page 197)

BOLLYWOOD BREAKFAST

East-Meets-Midwest Breakfast Bake (page 145)

Cucumber Raita (page 148)

Mango Lassi (page 200) or Creamy Coconut Chai (page 200)

LAZY SUMMER SUPPER

Strawberry-Basil Salad (page 59)

Beet-of-Your-Own Drummus Sandwiches (page 95)

Amazing Everything Cookies (page 174)

Raspberry Tea Syrup (page 199) with tea

ROMANTIC PICNIC

Figgy Blue Sandwiches (page 101)

Dijon Vegetable Toss (chilled) (page 111)

I'm So Mad About 'Stachio Cookies (page 168)

PRIZE-WINNING POTLUCK

Potluck Pasta Salad (page 65)

Three-Bean Salad (page 60)

Quick Pickled Onions (page 60)

Back-in-the-Day Date Bars (page 183)

COCKTAIL PARTY

Mushroom Pâté (page 40)

White Bean Basil Spread (page 39) with crudités

Rosemary Crisps (page 44)

Heavenly Sweet 'n' Savory Bites (page 47)

Herbed Garlic Polenta Fries (page 50)

Lemon Aioli (page 50)

IMPRESS-THE-PARENTS DINNER

Fast Lentil Salad (page 64)

Orecchiette with Creamy Tapenade (page 132)

Tahini Broccolini (page 108)

Fig Delight (page 193)

SIMPLY ELEGANT DINNER

Baked Tofu (page 143)

Pesto'd Potatoes (page 117)

Almond-Glazed Green Beans (page 113)

Best Cheesecake (page 177)

COZY COMFORT FOOD DINNER

Worknight's Shepherd's Pie (page 160)

Shallots and Spinach (page 109)

Fall Pumpkin Spice Cobbler (page 172)

GLUTEN-FREE FABULOUS DINNER

Roasted Carrot Risotto (page 125)

Roasted Green Onions (page 114)

Berry Balsamic Glaze (page 114)

Bananas for Gluten-Free Brownies (page 166)

Conversions

MEASURE	EQUIVALENT	METRIC
1 teaspoon	--	5.0 milliliters
1 tablespoon	3 teaspoons	14.8 milliliters
1 cup	16 tablespoons	236.8 milliliters
1 pint	2 cups	473.6 milliliters
1 quart	4 cups	947.2 milliliters
1 liter	4 cups + 3½ tablespoons	1,000 milliliters
1 ounce (dry)	2 tablespoons	28.35 grams
1 pound	16 ounces	453.49 grams
2.21 pounds	35.3 ounces	1 kilogram
325°F/350°F/375°F	--	165°C/177°C/190°C

Photo Credits

page 12 © Kris Cramer
page 15 © YummyBuum/shutterstock.com
page 17 © Kaidash/shutterstock.com
page 19 © Kris Cramer
page 22 © Kris Cramer
page 24 © Nata_Alhontess/shutterstock.com
page 29 © Kris Cramer
page 31 © Kris Cramer
page 33 © Kris Cramer
page 34 © Nata_Alhontess/shutterstock.com
page 36 © Kuzmina Aleksandra/shutterstock .com
page 37 © Mind Pixell/shutterstock.com
page 38 © Kris Cramer
page 40 © Sketch Master.ai/shutterstock.com
page 43 © Kris Cramer
page 45 © Sketch Master/shutterstock.com
page 46 © Kris Cramer
page 48 © Net Vector/shutterstock.com
page 51 © Kris Cramer
page 52 © Sketch Master/shutterstock.com
page 53 © alyaBigJoy/shutterstock.com
page 54 © Kris Cramer
page 57 © Kris Cramer
page 58 © Kris Cramer
page 61 © Kris Cramer
page 62 © Kris Cramer
page 64 © Jka/shutterstock.com
page 69 © Kris Cramer
page 72 © Kris Cramer
page 77 © Kris Cramer
page 79 © SuperArtWorks/shutterstock.com
page 80 © Kris Cramer
page 83 © Kris Cramer
page 84 © Epine/shutterstock.com
page 85 © Epine/shutterstock.com
page 86 © Sketch Master/shutterstock.com
page 88 © Kris Cramer
page 90 © Sketch Master/shutterstock.com
page 91 © More Vector/shutterstock.com
page 97 © Kris Cramer
page 98 © Babich Alexander/shutterstock.com
page 100 © Kris Cramer

page 102 © Iamnee/shutterstock.com
page 105 © Kris Cramer
page 107 © Kris Cramer
page 109 © Nata_Alhontess/shutterstock.com
page 111 © Sketch Master/shutterstock.com
page 112 © Kris Cramer
page 115 © Kris Cramer
page 116 © Nata_Alhontess/shutterstock.com
page 118 © Airin.dizain/shutterstock.com
page 120 © Kris Cramer
page 122 © Epine/shutterstock.com
page 127 © Kris Cramer
page 128 © Sketch Master/shutterstock.com
page 130 © Kris Cramer
page 132 © Olga_Zaripova/shutterstock.com
page 135 © Alena Kaz/shutterstock.com
page 136 © messer16/shutterstock.com
page 140 © Kris Cramer
page 142 © Sketch Master/shutterstock.com
page 143 © Sketch Master/shutterstock.com
page 147 © Kris Cramer
page 148 © Epine/shutterstock.com
page 149 © Epine/shutterstock.com
page 151 © Elena Pimonova/shutterstock.com
page 155 © Kris Cramer
page 156 © Kris Cramer
page 159 © Kris Cramer
page 161 © Sketch Master/shutterstock.com
page 163 © Kris Cramer
page 167 © Kris Cramer
page 169 © pikepicture/shutterstock.com
page 171 © Natalya Levish/shutterstock.com
page 174 © Sketch Master/shutterstock.com
page 175 © Kris Cramer
page 176 © Kris Cramer
page 180 © Kris Cramer
page 185 © Nata_Alhontess/shutterstock.com
page 189 © Kris Cramer
page 191 © Kris Cramer
page 193 © Epine/shutterstock.com
page 198 © Nikita Konashenko/shutterstock.com

Recipe Index

Acknowledgments

This book was a long time coming. Now, after spreading lots of TJ's love and being asked to write a "cook" book for years, here it is. To all of my blog and book readers, my thanks are endless!

Many thanks to my friends and family for your love and support—and for not "unfriending" me after months of food-related updates with varying levels of panic and joy. A special thanks to Ted Schatz for allowing me to take over his kitchen (and fridge), to Ben Schatz for being my sounding board and human garbage disposal, to Dylan Norcross for keeping me company during epic cooking sessions, and to Alec Gaige for enduring *many* trips to Trader Joe's.

A giant thanks to all of my recipe testers: Jeannie Barnes, Emma Bates, Courtney Blair, Tiffany Cadiz, Marlene and Bobby Gaige, Niki Jay, Jessica Auxier, Jennifer Katz, Susan Kaufman, Abby Ledford, Sara Leier Horwath, Clea Mahoney, Romina Martucci, Chrissy Mills, Jenni Mischel, Brenda Monteleone, Christina and Ken Mott, Karen and Brian Reiter, Leigh Saluzzi, and Jennifer Stacie. A very special thanks goes out to super-tester Ana Lucas, who is a goddess among foodies.

Thanks to the good folks at Ulysses Press for believing in me and for making this project happen. And I would be remiss if I didn't thank all of the Hawaiian shirts at all of the TJ's stores that I have frequented over the years.

About the Author

KRIS CRAMER is a vegan baker, blogger, and author. Under the name Kris Holechek Peters, she authored *The 100 Best Vegan Baking Recipes* and *Have Your Cake and Vegan Too*, and is the writer of nomnomnomblog.com and noshnoshnosh.com. She lives in the Midwest with her three cats, two kids, and an embarrassingly large number of specialty baking pans.